THROUGH A YOUNG BOY'S EYES

A Memoir of Appalachia in the 1960s

THROUGH A YOUNG BOY'S EYES

A Memoir of Appalachia in the 1960s

James F. Simpson

EXCELLER BOOKS™
A GLOBAL PRESS

Through A Young Boy's Eyes
A Memoir of Appalachia in the 1960s

Copyright ©, James F. Simpson, USA, 2022

ISBN: 978-93-93734-02-0

First published in India in 2022 by Exceller Books

G1, Dream Apartment, Degree College Road, Belgharia, Kolkata, 700056, India

www.excellerbooks.com

Dedication

This narrative would not have been written without the encouragement of my wife of forty-two years, Kimberly Hanger Simpson. This book is dedicated to my family still living and to the memory of my beloved family members who have passed from this earth but remain alive in my heart and mind.

Acknowledgement

I acknowledge with gratitude and thank my European ancestors who demonstrated that a fulfilling life could be made with courage, ingenuity, hard work, perseverance, spirituality, and an unwavering devotion to family. And to all those whom I have encountered during this journey of life who educated, inspired, encouraged, and loved me, I am forever indebted.

Preface

This book is an account of a family living in the deeply-forested Appalachian Mountains during the 1960s; the culture reflected in the pages that follow generally mirrors the norms of the coal-fields region of Appalachia during this decade. Although all the characters in this novel are fictional, the writing was heavily influenced by my own childhood spent in the Appalachian region of the country. The views of the characters do not represent my personal opinions or beliefs.

I strove to write the book filtered through the lens of a young boy's eyes, endeavoring to include adult perspectives only when necessary to capture the context of the story. Readers may well find some of the language offensive and antithetical to American values. Accounts of blatant racism are reflected in the book, along with a young boy's struggle to reconcile why segregation and discrimination even existed.

Having been an educator, parent, and grandparent, I have learned that children have unique outlooks on the world around them that often are in conflict with those of the adults in their lives. I never cease to be amazed, and often am amused and delighted, when gaining new insight into children's views and perspectives of their world.

James Franklin Simpson
2022

Table of Contents

1/ Creekside School

"Get up! Get up! You have to go to school today!" I was startled by the frantic, yet commanding, voice of my mother. Unsure of whether I was dreaming or being forced from the warmth and comfort of my bed, I pulled the quilt over my shoulders and burrowed my body tightly into the covers, choosing to believe that it was all an unpleasant dream. The colorful quilt, which was hand-stitched by my mother from clothing remnants, reliably provided safety and security. Tiny brown specks of dried blood, barely visible to the naked eye, dotted the quilt in places where Mom's fingers were unable to avoid the piercings of a needle during the hundreds of through-and-back stitches that were necessary to attach the quilted top pieces to muslin backing.

My bewilderment was evident to Mom as she approached my bedside a second time, only to find me still huddled beneath the quilt. She continued to shout, "Get up! I said, 'Get up!'" and began to shake my upper torso so hard that all question of experiencing a really bad dream was removed. Reluctantly, I pulled the covers away from my body and sat on the side of the bed looking for my shorts and shirt that Mom had carefully hung on the foot post; both were still there waiting for me to put on before I located my socks and shoes. As I removed the clothes from the foot post of the bed, I was drawn to the ornamental curves in the wood crafted by my Dad on his lathe. I recalled watching with anticipation as Dad would turn the pine board round and round to allow the tool to penetrate the wood, deeply changing its dimensions; it brought to life a sculptured piece of art ready for a couple of coats of a dark varnish stain. The pungent odor of the varnish was still pronounced two years after the twin-size bed had been completed and added to the small room where my two older brothers shared a slightly larger bed.

My older brothers were already up and dressed and sitting at the kitchen table eating their breakfast of warm Quaker oats smothered with as much butter and granulated sugar as they could add in order to mask the pasty taste of oatmeal. Johnny would begin the eighth grade of school this year and was ribbing Ronnie that that day marked the beginning of his last year of graded elementary at Creekside School. No lament was evident in any of Johnny's boastful exchanges, reminding Ronnie that after that school year he no longer would have to get out of bed an hour early in order for Dad to be the first teacher to arrive at Creekside School as the head teacher, ride in the back seat of a Studebaker station wagon with his two nagging brothers scrunched in beside him, and be seen by the other kids in the neighborhood carrying his lunch in a brown paper bag that showed the wear and tear of being recycled for days at a time. Ronnie, being quick-witted and always on the offensive to poke fun, could not resist reminding Johnny that even though he would be privileged to ride the school bus to and from high school next year, along with my sister Debbie, the pretty girls would not want to sit next to him and look at his acne. As the banter had now escalated to a new level that was overheard by Dad dressing in an adjacent room, the brothers quickly gulped down as many bites of oatmeal as possible as Dad made his way into the kitchen and admonished Johnny and Ronnie to knock it off and go on to the car.

As I realized the entertainment provided by my brothers had ended, Mom came into my room and saw that I had not yet dressed for school. "Get your clothes on right now while I find your socks and shoes!" she fussed. I dressed quickly, realizing that I needed to get to the bathroom soon. Mom brought the socks and shoes to me with a sense of urgency. "You're going to cause your Dad to be late for the first day of school and he won't be happy," she said while tugging at my foot to insert it into the dark brown, lace-up shoe. "Hurry up!" she said. "You haven't eaten breakfast or brushed your teeth, and your Dad is ready to leave now." I managed to get both of my shoes on and tied and sleepily started toward the door to make my way outside to the privy. "Stop! You come back here now!" Mom shouted. When I told Mom that I had to go to the bathroom immediately or I would wet my pants, she relented with the admonishment that I hurry as fast as possible in order to get back to the house to eat breakfast and brush my teeth.

A trip to the outdoor privy was always an adventure. The structure was located sixty yards or so from the front door of the house; the rough pine boards that covered the sides had been painted over the summer with creosote containing a dark green dye, and the smell of the coal tar still permeated the air. Frankly, the smell of the creosote was a much-preferred stench when compared with that of uric acid and methane gas. As I entered the privy, I was startled to hear my sister Debbie exclaim, "Go away! I'm in here." I quickly exited, but not before letting her know that she needed to hurry because I really needed to use the toilet quickly. In what seemed like a half-hour but was only a few minutes, Debbie left the privy to return to the house, but not before scowling at me in passing. I quickly relieved myself and made my way back to the house. Mom met me at the door reminding me to wash my hands and brush my teeth.

Our small bathroom housed a bathtub and lavatory sink, both of which sported a blue porcelain finish. I tried to squeeze what little toothpaste remained of an almost-empty tube, all the while hearing Mom shouting, "Hurry! Hurry up in there!" As I left the bathroom, she met me at the door with my lunch bag and a to-go biscuit breakfast that had been left over from dinner the night before. "You don't have time to eat oatmeal and you need to get something on your stomach," she said while kissing me on the forehead and ushering me out the door at the same time. With everything in tow, I hurriedly ran to the car that already was loaded with my Dad and two brothers. As Ronnie pulled me into the back seat of the station wagon, I thought of how lucky my younger brother Benny was that he was too young to have to get up early and go to school.

Miss Margaret, whom I knew from attending our church, would be joining us on our ride to school today, having been appointed this school year (1960-61) as the teacher of the one-room school house at Dunn Stop. We would be dropping her off a mile or so before we reached Creekside School. Miss Margaret was a beautiful woman with long, flowing black hair; she smelled of flowery perfume and cinnamon from the Dentyne gum she chewed. We boys would smile and giggle, whispering to each other that our Mom might be jealous of Miss Margaret sitting in the front seat of the car with Dad.

As Dad turned west on Highway 68, the valleys and streams became more visible. It was early September in 1960, and leaves had begun to fall. The highway pavement, still wet from last night's rain, showcased the flattened yellow and red maple leaves. Water flowed forcefully and abundantly over the rocks in the streams, completely filling the width of the stream beds. Approaching Martin's Gap, one had a panoramic view of the modest but well-kept houses that sprinkled the landscape outlining the streets. The flat bottom land, on which the houses were situated, was flanked by the beautiful mountains and my rear-seat window in the car seemed to frame the scene perfectly in my mind. In the hills and mountains of Roane County, bottom land was a large, flat portion of acreage beside a stream or river and was at a premium because of the mountainous terrain.

As the road meandered on toward its eventual end, a straight stretch of highway took us past Dr. Wilson's mansion. Dr. Wilson was a beloved physician who was schooled up East and came to Western Virginia in the early 1900s to serve as a local coal company's doctor. After a few years of medical practice, he was able to purchase an interest in a coal mine and successfully managed a mining operation for many years. Dr. Wilson did not cease practicing medicine once he became a businessman; patients from multiple generations sought medical care from the doctor and he operated a small office practice from his home until shortly before his death.

The expansive Wilson estate was situated on bottom land and enclosed by a black, wrought iron fence; the lush mountainside foliage provided a fitting backdrop to the red brick mansion and meticulously landscaped lawn. I had never experienced such a view in three dimensions. Pictures in some of Dad's books and backdrops to programs viewed on our black-and-white-picture television were no comparison for what I was seeing. Fascinated, I pleaded with Dad, "Could we go by this house more slowly when we drive back home today?"

We soon made our way to the tiny Dunn Stop School where we would drop Miss Margaret off to begin her first day of school. As she gathered her things and began to make her way out of the car, Dad reminded her that he would not be returning to pick her up for the return trip until well after 5:00 p.m. because there would be work for him to do after school. As we told Miss Margaret goodbye, she looked back at us saying, "Boys, be good at school today and I might have some gum for you this afternoon."

As Dad pulled his car into the parking lot, I cast my eyes on the white clapboard building that appeared much larger than the Dunn Stop School. Dad and my brothers had told me that there were four classrooms at Creekside School - one room housing grade one, another housing grade two, a third housing grades three, four and five, and Dad's room housing grades six, seven and eight. The school had no cafeteria and no designated room for a library or physical education. A small playground on one side of the building had swings, a large metal slide, and a see-saw. A basketball court was located next to the parking area with hardened dirt serving as its surface; it had several puddles of muddy water on it today due to last night's rain.

No sooner had Dad parked the car and turned off the ignition than Johnny and Ronnie bounded from the vehicle, leaving me alone in the back seat. My trepidation of being in a new and unfamiliar place suddenly was very real as I longed to be back home eating my breakfast and taking as much time as I wanted. "Dad, I want to go back home," I whimpered Dad turned in his seat; he smiled at me and assured me that he would be with me that day. We exited the car, and then ascended the wide, wooden steps to the porch landing of Dad's classroom. My father's tall, brawny build presented a commanding presence that reassured me that everything would be OK. Dad unlocked the door and ushered me inside to a chair at a small table near a window. He brought me a small paper carton containing one-half pint of white milk to drink. As I opened the milk carton, I saw other children playing on the swings on the side of the building housing the playground and could hear the laughter and excitement. "I think I might like being on the playground," I thought to myself.

Dad soon told me it was time to go to my classroom and meet my new teacher, Mrs. Faulkner. We walked back to the porch and down the landing to another classroom with the door open. As we entered the room, I was introduced to Mrs. Faulkner and invited to sit at a desk along with other boys and girls who already were in the classroom. After all the parents had left the room, Mrs. Faulkner asked us to say our names and "hello" aloud to the other kids. We sang songs and listened to stories until we were asked to form a line to go outside for recess. Recess seemed to help me release any remaining anxiety due to my new experience and I was delighted to join the other kids running around in circles on the playground. "If you run around and around lots of times, you'll get really dizzy," another boy exclaimed. Accepting the challenge, I almost fell against a banister post before hearing the clanging of a large bell signaling that playtime had ended.

I found my way back to the classroom, along with the other boys and girls, and took my seat. Mrs. Faulkner ensured that everyone had returned to their desks. One boy sitting behind me was crying uncontrollably. Mrs. Faulkner tried her best to console and inveigle him by placing a cherry red, paper-back primer on his desk; although he smiled after being given the book, his crying continued along with faint whispers of "I want to go home."

Mrs. Faulkner proceeded to distribute the readers to all the children. How excited I was to have my very own book, with a bright red cover and a picture of a boy who resembled me, a girl with her hair in pigtails, and a dog with a big coat of hair and a bushy tail. The book, *My Little Red Story Book*, would be the first of three primer readers to which I would be introduced in first grade. The Ginn and Company reading series had been adopted by the county school district and was used in all the elementary schools.

Calling the class's attention, Mrs. Faulkner began her introduction of Tom, Betty, Flip and Pony. Holding up a large cardboard cutout of the boy pictured on the front of the book, my teacher wore a huge smile as she announced, "Boys and girls, I would like for you to meet Tom." Tom's sister Betty, the girl with her hair in pigtails was introduced, along with the dog, Flip, and the horse, Pony. The excitement of everyone was palpable as the teacher circulated among us students allowing each an opportunity to see the figures up close; some of the kids reached out for a touch. Although I, too, wanted to touch the figures, remembering Dad's admonition that I should not touch anything that did not belong to me while at school or I would be in trouble caused me to refrain. Throughout much of the rest of the morning, Mrs. Faulkner read to the class frequently reminding us that we, ourselves, soon would be reading about Tom, Betty, Flip and Pony from our new books.

Lunch period arrived and everyone was allowed to go to the playground or remain in the classroom to eat. The small cartons of milk, just like the one Dad had given me in his classroom, were distributed to all the boys and girls who had brought two cents from home to purchase a drink. I noticed that several classmates of mine did not purchase milk and instead were removing small bottles of Coca Cola from their lunch bags. I thought of how much better the cola would taste as compared to the white milk. Carrying my lunch bag and milk, I made my way outside to find a spot to sit and have lunch. A boy and a girl I recognized, both of whom were in my class, were sitting on the top of a rock wall that was built to stabilize the earth and prevent it from eroding into the stream that flowed below it. The girl called out, "Thomas Lee, do you want to sit with us?" I replied in the affirmative by nodding my head and sat on the wall opening my bag to see what Mom had packed for me to eat. There was a bologna sandwich wrapped in waxed paper along with a Moon Pie. I was envious of the girl, who was eating a ham sandwich and had placed an oatmeal cream pie next to her milk. I would have loved to have eaten the oatmeal pie instead of the Moon Pie, and I even contemplated asking the girl if we could trade pies. The boy was enjoying his Coca-Cola after adding a small package of peanuts to its contents, which I thought to be a strange thing to do. I ate about half of the sandwich, washing it down with the cold white milk before joining the other kids on the playground.

The large, metal slide was the biggest I had ever seen. I carefully studied its height and ladder before finding the courage to try it out. Three-fourths of the way up the ladder I looked down, while waiting for the kid in front of me to make it to the top, and was immediately overcome with anxiety. "Maybe I need to climb down and not do this," I silently pondered. Catching a glance of two other kids climbing up the ladder behind me, I knew that I had no choice but to climb to the top and go down the ladder. With my bottom firmly planted on the top of the slide and my hands clinging to both sides, I pushed myself off feeling the force of the wind in my face and the euphoria of experiencing my small body in motion. It was as though I was flying in the air, and I did not want to accept that I had made it to the bottom and that my feet were planted back on the ground. "That was fun!" I excitedly remarked to another boy who had made it down the slide earlier.

Before I could get in line for another turn on the slide, the large bell sounded, once again announcing that the lunch period had ended. I ran back to the steps and walked into the classroom to take my seat. I was very thirsty and had begun to sweat as a result of my activity on the playground and the dramatic rise in temperature since the beginning of the school day. Mrs. Faulkner allowed the classroom door to remain open along with three large windows located on the side of the room; she had placed a large fan near the door to provide air circulation. After everyone was seated and accounted for, we were allowed to form a line to have a drink of water. The sink, with an extra-large white porcelain-coated basin, had a big spigot that had been turned on by the teacher to allow each boy and girl to use a small, cone-shaped paper cup to have a drink of water. The boy in front of me filled his cup three times and I decided it was OK for me to do so as well.

Back in my seat, I was pleased to hear the teacher announce that everyone could put their heads down on the top of the desks to rest while she read a story. The boy seated in the row behind me was no longer crying as Mrs. Faulkner had approached him before beginning to read and announced to the class, "I'm glad Billy is feeling better." Listening to every word of the story while fighting the urge to doze off, I imagined myself back home in my bed taking a nap after enjoying a grilled cheese sandwich for lunch. At some point, I apparently had been unable to escape sleep as I was surprised to hear singing voices. Being startled, I managed to get my head off the top of the desk and raise it quickly to not draw any additional attention to myself. Mrs. Faulkner gave me a glancing smile as she continued leading the class in singing, "...This old man. He played four. He played knick knack on my door. With a knick knack, paddy whack, give a dog a bone. This old man came rolling home...."

The classroom singing ended shortly and my teacher distributed an additional new book to everyone that she called an arithmetic workbook. I quickly recognized my name, "Thomas Lee," written on the front of the book in a space that had two straight lines on the top and bottom and a hatched line between them. As I opened the book to look inside, I heard the teacher instruct, "Boys and girls, if you have brought a pencil with you today, do not use it to write in your book now. We will be writing in the book throughout the year as we learn about numbers." I closed the book to focus my attention back on Mrs. Faulkner's instruction but not without wondering about the picture I had seen that looked exactly like the two large objects located beside the long board on the wall at the front of the classroom. Colorful balls that appeared to be made of wood were stretched across long metal rods; there were rows and rows of them attached to a brown frame.

Once again, everyone was asked to line up to go outside for another recess. I returned to the playground area but was feeling too tired to try out the big slide a second time. I wondered how much longer it would be before Dad would be taking us back home. I caught sight of Johnny and Ronnie playing basketball on the earthen court. The sun and heat of the day had caused most of the puddles of water to disappear from the area. Walking back toward my classroom after hearing the bell sound, I saw not one, but two privies, located adjacent to one another with boys lined up waiting to go inside one and girls awaiting their turn at the other.

After recess ended, everyone was asked to sit on the floor in a circle; everyone observed Mrs. Faulkner with interest while she distributed red, plastic discs. Waiting for everyone to receive their allotment, I was absorbed in pretending that the discs were quarters and that I was now rich. Everyone was asked to pick up one disc and to hold it in our hand with our arm extended high into the air. "Everyone has one shiny disc," Mrs. Faulkner proclaimed. We were asked to pick up a second disc with the other hand and hold it in the air while continuing to hold the first disc. "Do you still have only one disc?" the teacher asked to which most of the class replied to a resounding "No!" "You now have two discs," she affirmed. I quickly made the connection to buying an oatmeal cookie at Smith's Grocery. After telling Mr. Smith that I wanted to buy an oatmeal cookie from his big glass jar on the counter, he would say, "I need two pennies for one cookie, Thomas Lee." I would then dig into my pocket and place all my pennies on the glass counter, allowing Mr. Smith to take two of them before telling me to put the remainder back in my pocket. If I happened to have several pennies, without fail Mr. Smith would ask if I was sure I only wanted to buy one cookie. The arithmetic lesson continued for an hour or so longer before the bell sounded, signaling that the school day had ended. Mrs. Faulkner reminded us to place our reading and arithmetic books in the space located underneath our desks before telling everyone goodbye and that she hoped to see us all again tomorrow.

Johnny was standing outside my classroom door as I made my way to the porch landing. "Tom told me to come and get you; you have to go with me back to his room and wait with Ronnie and me until we are ready to go home," Johnny said. Debbie, Johnny and Ronnie referred to my Dad as Tom in that he was their stepfather, as explained to Benny and me by our Mom. I didn't understand why all my siblings didn't call my father "Dad," but in deference to my Mom's explanation, I accepted it without question. After what seemed like hours, Dad was finished with his work, and we were ready to go home.

Upon getting myself situated in the car between my two brothers, I found myself overcome with fatigue and hunger and anxious to arrive home. Dad stopped at the Dunn Stop School to pick up Miss Margaret, who was awaiting our arrival on the school's front porch; she checked to make sure she had secured the big metal latch lock on the door before making her way to our car. Once inside the car, Miss Margaret offered each of us a stick of Dentyne gum which was gratefully accepted with a "Thank you" from all. As we made our way down the highway, Dad encountered a car on the opposite side of the road that was careening toward us. Steering our car quickly to the shoulder of the road, Dad was able to avoid what could have been a serious mishap. As I began to doze off, I continued to hear Miss Margaret and Dad discussing that the driver of the out-of-control vehicle was most likely drunk.

We soon arrived at the junction of Highway 68 and US 24 where Bascom Jones operated a service station. Dad stopped for gasoline and got outside of the car to talk with Mr. Jones while he was pumping the gas. Mr. Jones, who was wearing a button-up shirt with a logo affixed, and appeared to be an amiable man, was someone whom Dad knew to be his friend. While waiting, I found myself overtaken with the wafting smell of French fries and hamburgers that were being prepared inside the building. I asked Miss Margaret if anyone could get a hamburger and French fries at the service station. She replied, "Oh yes. They sell hamburgers, hotdogs, French fries and other foods at a diner counter inside the store." "What's a diner counter?" I asked. After answering my question, Miss Margaret went on to explain in detail how the burgers and fries were prepared. With my hunger now exacerbated, I imagined myself at lunch eating a delicious cheeseburger wrapped in waxed paper, along with hot fries smothered with ketchup, and washing it all down with a Coca-Cola, quite a contrast to the bologna sandwich I had eaten earlier.

As we approached the road where we would turn to go to my grandparents' house, I noticed the car slowing considerably. Several cars appeared to be totally stopped on the highway in front of us. Dad announced that the train had stopped on the tracks that crossed the road in front of us. With a tired body and a full bladder, I was relieved to see the train begin moving again after ten minutes or so. Ronnie began counting the empty gondolas, or open-topped freight cars, that were enroute to the coal mines a mile or so away; he announced that over one hundred had passed, before the train exited the highway and the cars began to move once again. After dropping Miss Margaret off, we soon arrived home, where I climbed over Ronnie to exit the car and run to the privy.

Making my way back to the house, I washed my hands and found everyone already seated at the kitchen table enjoying a delicious dinner that had been prepared by my mother and sister, Debbie. I devoured my serving of meat loaf made with onion soup mix, fried potatoes, and made-from-scratch biscuits and did my best to pretend to be eating the green beans. Observing my antics, Dad sternly said, "You're not getting up from this table until you eat more of those green beans." The dishes were soon washed and put away and Debbie was calling for Benny and me to report to the bathroom to take our baths. With my bath taken and teeth having been brushed, I soon was ready for bed. I had no trouble falling asleep, yet I was surprised that I actually was anticipating being awakened early the next day to return to Creekside School.

My second-grade teacher at Creekside School, Miss Morgan, had been Mom's teacher years earlier at a different school. My younger brother, Benny and I had heard the stories of our mother walking to school in the early 1930s, and of her teachers, of whom Miss Morgan was a favorite. Benny joined our school crew in 1961, and, along with me, was a student in Miss Morgan's split-grades classroom. Miss Morgan always had an ample supply of Jergen's hand lotion in a large, pump-action bottle on her desk and insisted that her students use it after washing their hands. Her classroom was equipped with a huge, pot-bellied stove that was surrounded by a screen, made of large sheets of asbestos, designed to absorb some of the intense heat radiating from the unit. She often allowed other students and me to assist her using a hexagraph device to make copies of tests. The master copy, completed with a special pencil, was placed at the top of a tray of a solidified gel-like substance that would imprint the markings of the pencil. Individual sheets of typing paper would be pressed on the tray and peeled off making a printing of the master copy. Making fifteen copies could easily take thirty minutes or so but was a welcomed reprieve to a young boy who was relegated to spend most of his day in a cramped seat.

One cold, wintry day a classmate asked Miss Morgan if he could be excused to go to the toilet. Miss Morgan replied, "Yes, but make sure you put on your coat before going out in the cold.

You need to hurry back and wash your hands, so you won't miss our reading group's share time." The boy was gone for an extended period, prompting the teacher to call me to her desk and ask if I would go out to the privy to check on the classmate. Bundling up in my coat, I made my way to the boys' privy and knocked on the door; there was no acknowledgement from anyone inside. I knocked again, calling the boy's name, and still heard no response. As it was getting colder with the bitter wind blowing, I made one last attempt to summon a response. "Miss Morgan said to tell you to come back inside the school now!" I asserted with my voice trembling from the cold. Opening the door of the privy while simultaneously sobbing, my classmate appeared. "What's wrong?" I asked. "I dropped my toboggan cap down the toilet and don't know how to get it out. I'll be in bad trouble with my Dad for losing it," he replied while continuing to whimper. "You can't get it out of the toilet; it's dirty down there," I told the boy. I finally convinced the classmate to return to the building with me by promising him that I would tell Miss Morgan what happened and ask her to help him not get into trouble with his Dad.

Miss Carnes taught my third-grade class. She was a very young teacher who had completed some of her college training and was eligible for a conditional teaching license; her classroom consisted of grades three, four, and five. Miss Carnes was a pretty lady who often would sit on the wooden steps of the school to supervise students on the playground at recess; wearing bobby socks and loafers; one easily could have mistaken her for one of the eighth-grade girls. Miss Carnes loved music and incorporated it into the curriculum for all three grades. I always was excited when my teacher would allow each of the grades to transition from their segregated studies to participate in a joint lesson like music.

In early spring, the vegetation emerged from its winter dormancy to paint the mountains and valleys with a palette of green. Everyone looked forward to springtime, so we could be outdoors after the school day had ended. Billy, a boy in the fifth grade, had spent Sunday afternoon with his family gathering wild leeks, commonly known as ramps, in the meadow by the church.

Billy arrived at school on Monday still emitting the pungent garlic smell, having eaten his fill of ramps the day before. It didn't take long for my classmates to raise their hand and ask, "Miss Carnes, what is that awful smell? Something stinks in here." Or to simply blurt out, "That stink is going to make me throw up!" Miss Carnes did her best to calm the storm, but the discomfort of her students continued to forcefully be expressed. I glanced over in the direction of the smell and saw that Billy was now sobbing with Miss Carnes whispering in his ear. Shortly thereafter, Billy gathered his belongings, put on his jacket, and left the room for his short walk home from school. All the students at the school, except my brothers and me, lived in the Creekside community and were able to walk to and from the building.

I never got tired of attending Creekside School and learned to enjoy the long commute. During the evening trip home, Dad purposely would slow the car down on the long stretch of road that ran parallel to Dr. Wilson's beautiful home, allowing my brothers and me to fantasize about how much fun we could have in the expansive yard. Every so often my father would tell us interesting stories about brave Indian warriors who risked their own safety to protect their families. These tales helped the time seem to pass more quickly during the long ride home.

2 / The Family

The community of Dawson, where I grew up, was settled by European immigrants, most of whom made their way to the wilderness of Virginia from North Carolina, Pennsylvania and Tennessee in the eighteenth and nineteenth centuries. The terrain of the mountains was rough, requiring the early settlers to make their way into the area by navigating the stream beds in the valleys. The Dawson family, after whom the hamlet was named, had immigrated to the United States from England, clearing and settling the fertile land that was relatively flat and located near a good supply of water. Having brought seeds, farm animals, and packhorses with them to the valley, they were able to create sustainable farms in a short period of time. The Dawsons, along with many other families, took advantage of the flat land located up old Sulpher Creek to stake out a living from the land. Early census records enumerated a large number of siblings living in each household more than likely bred, in part, to ensure that an adequate supply of farm help readily was available.

Mom's parents were direct descendants of the Poe and Lewis clans. The Poes, who settled in Dawson, came from Ireland to the United States, first arriving in North Carolina to work in the tobacco fields; their families back in Ireland had introduced them to small cottages with hard, earthen floors, small windows, and thatched roofs. The early Poe residents of Dawson were no strangers to primitive living and hard lives. The Lewises, eventually making their way into Roane County, Virginia, came to America from England, living first in the state of Pennslyvania before settling much of the available flat land located closer to the town of New Castle, then known as Rockcastle.

Dad's parents were descendants of the Browns and Bratchers. The Bratchers were European immigrants who eventually settled in the Virginia area close to Roanoke. My paternal ancestors first lived in Salem County, Virginia, near the towns of Morrisville and Cedartown. According to my grandfather, my great-grandfather Brown became a "read" lawyer in Pike County, Virginia, in the late 1800s, practicing the profession without having a formal law school education; this practice, most famously associated with Abraham Lincoln, was allowed by the state of Virginia as one would independently read and study the law before being examined by the Court and given the authorization to practice. According to my grandfather, his father had mishandled a divorce proceeding in the early 1900s; having to flee Pike County to avoid legal prosecution, he moved to West Virginia to work in the coal mines, taking my fourteen-year-old grandfather with him.

My mother, Margaret Poe Brown, spent her formative years in the community of Sulpher Creek, located along US 24, near the state of Tennessee border; her father was a veteran of World War I who farmed and worked as a carpenter for the Sulpher Creek Coal Company, while her mother managed all the family responsibilities of cooking, cleaning, caring for the children, and assisting with light farming duties. In addition to Mom, there were seven other siblings in the household. I would listen intently to a vivid account of what everyday life was like growing up in a large family and especially enjoyed Mom's burst of animation as she would say, "I always looked forward to going with my Momma and papa to the new ground to tend the vegetable garden." Mom's elaborate recounting of killing and preparing hogs, placing hams in the smokehouse for curing, assisting her mother in making lye soap from pork renderings, and gathering eggs in the hen house would captivate me for long periods of time; she was terrified of snakes and would frequently take advantage of her encounter with a large snake near the hen house on her parents' property to caution my siblings and me to be on guard for the avoid-at-all-costs reptile.

Mom's formal education ended at Camden High School during which time she made the decision to marry without the blessing of her parents; her first marriage would produce three children: Debbie, Johnny, and Ronnie. My mother had told me that she filed for divorce and received custody of her children only a few years into the union.

My father, Green Thomas Brown, grew up in the coal mining camp of Coalgap, named after the black, sedimentary rock that was extracted daily from the huge seams underground. His father was a life-long coal miner, first entering the long, underground tunnels as a teenager in West Virginia. Having spent the majority of his occupational career mining coal in Roane County, my paternal grandfather was a first-hand witness to unsafe working conditions and unjust compensation; he was an early member and long-time advocate for the United Mine Workers of America, continuing his service as an elected officer during his retirement years. My grandmother spent her life as a wife and caregiver for her children, while managing all the household tasks undeterred by periodic bouts of mental depression. In addition to Dad, there were two other siblings, Charlotte and William, both of whom would go on as adults to earn bachelor's degrees in journalism and civil engineering respectively; they would remain a part of my Dad's life into adulthood.

Dad contracted a rare virus as a child, resulting in his heart being permanently damaged. In spite of his physical limitations, he was an active boy playing on one of the first organized football teams at Camden High School; however, unlike his brother William, who served in the United States Navy, he was deemed medically unqualified to serve in the military. I often found amusement in looking at an old photograph of Dad and his teammates donning helmets made of leather without chin guards and comparing them to those worn by the Green Bay Packers whom I would see on the television on Sunday afternoon. Dad completed three years of in-residence study at Western Virginia Teachers' College in the mid-1940s, which qualified him for a temporary teaching certificate. Mom often recounted to her children the struggle that Dad had faced in paying his tuition and living expenses while enrolled in college; this included selling his blood and taking any odd job he could find in the Raidertown area. Dad completed the requirements for his bachelor's degree by attending summer school, graduating in the late 1950s. Prior to his current assignment as head teacher at Creekside School, my father had served as a teacher at Lee School, located at Sulpher Creek, which was attended by my mother and all her siblings.

Dad's first marriage ended in divorce and there were no children born to the union. Mom was working as a server at Johnson's Café in downtown Harveytown when she first met her future husband. According to Mom's account, Dad frequented the restaurant, always offering her a smile. The story was always accentuated with Mom noting, "And he always left me a really good tip."

Mom and Dad, along with Debbie, Johnny, and Ronnie, moved into a house in the early 1950s that Dad had purchased during his first marriage. The property was located in an area of Dawson accessed by a one-and-a-half-lane road that wound around a blind curve up a hill. The modest white clapboard structure housed six rooms: a kitchen with a large table situated in the middle of the room; a two-piece bathroom with a tub and lavatory sink; a living room; and three small bedrooms. A large porch with a very comfortable swing was located on the southern side of the house. A coal stove for heating the entire house was in the living room and small, one-over-one-hung windows had been installed in most of the rooms.

Without exception, our family ate dinner together every evening. While Benny and I enjoyed playing outside, Johnny and Ronnie completed homework and chores; Dad often would catch a quick nap while Debbie and Mom prepared the meal. One evening, Mom had served beef liver and onions, mashed potatoes, peas, and cornbread. I had arrived at the table very tired from a day at school and playing a game of chase outdoors. My disappointment and sullen face at seeing liver on the table was without doubt observed by my mother. Turning to me Mom declared, "You will give our thanks tonight." I replied, "I'll say a silent one." I was in no mood for the tone of my voice to be perceived as being disrespectful to God. Everyone bowed their heads, and I quickly breathed a prayer under my breath before ending my petition with an "Amen." Dishes of food were passed, and I placed some of each on my plate, taking only a small amount of liver. The mashed potatoes and peas were always tasty and I speedily ate both servings. I began to nibble on the slice of corn bread, being careful to only bite off a few crumbs each time hoping that everyone else would finish dinner and I would be excused from the table. My scheme was exposed as I heard my Dad say, "Thomas Lee, you need to eat your liver. If you and Benny will eat your liver, I'll give you a nickel to purchase a Brown Cow at Jack Smith's store." Mom amplified Dad's enticing offer by adding, "The liver is full of vitamins that will make you grow big and strong, so go ahead and get started." The thoughts of eating the crunchy, chocolate coating on the ice cream bar was a powerful motivator for a young boy who was not afforded such delights very often. Cutting a small piece of the liver with my fork, I dipped it in the mashed potatoes and placed it in my mouth. The more I chewed the liver, the queasier I felt; finally I was able to swallow the first bite. Seeing what had occurred, Mom complimented me, encouraging me to continue eating. As I cut the second portion, I felt the urge to regurgitate. Knowing that I could not swallow another bite of the liver, I plotted what I thought would turn out to be an infallible strategy for making the liver disappear along with other distasteful foods that would be served to me in the future.

Placing the second bite of the liver in my mouth, I began to pulverize it with my teeth to get the consistency to an almost liquid form. I raised my napkin over my mouth, pretending to cough, as I spat the liver into it. Moving the napkin back to my lap, I began to transfer the food to the large crack that I had felt under the wooden table; the crack easily accommodated all the food and I continued to repeat the process. I had glanced at Benny's plate seeing that he had made little progress with respect to eating his serving of liver. Mom had taken notice and once again and complimented and encouraged me to continue eating. It soon became more difficult to stuff the liver in the crack prompting me to ask Dad, "I've eaten a lot of the liver. May I be excused to go to the store for my Brown Cow?" With a broad smile Dad exclaimed, "I'm really surprised!" while nodding "Yes" to me and pulling the coin out of the pocket on his trousers. I took the nickel and made my way out the front door in a flash.

Walking the block or so to Smith's Grocery, I fantasized about the delicious taste of the chocolate and ice cream in my mouth. It would be quite a contrast to the fetid liver that had almost caused me to vomit in my plate. I entered the store, asked

Mr. Smith for a Brown Cow, and gave him my nickel. I was enjoying the ice cream bar exceedingly as I made my way around the corner not far from the house. As I saw my brother Ronnie walking toward me, my heart seemed to stop, sensing that my plan had been exposed and that I was in big trouble. Remaining silent, I heard Ronnie's voice project, "Boy, are you in big trouble with Tom! The liver fell out of the table." Meeting me at the door, Dad took me in one of the bedrooms and meted out a punishment which left me with a stinging bottom.

A year or more later, I accompanied Mom to the grocery store and was perusing the meat counter while she was moving up and down the aisles shopping. I spotted the plastic-wrapped packages of beef liver, which for some uncanny reason seemed appealing and appetizing. Being somewhat surprised, I lingered at the counter intently gazing at the liver hoping that a familiar repulsive, nauseating feeling would transpire; instead, the thought of eating the liver smothered with the onion flavoring was even more palatable. Locating Mom in one of the aisles, I asked, "Will you buy some of the beef liver and serve it for dinner? I promise I'll eat it." Bewildered and amused she retorted, "I'm too busy shopping for your jokes. I know you won't eat liver." I persisted with the nagging and Mom made her way to the meat counter to put the liver in her cart. "I'll have the liver for dinner tonight and you'll eat it or be in trouble with your Dad and me," she admonished. To her amazement, I enjoyed a serving of liver for dinner that evening and continued to enjoy it whenever it was served.

The three bedrooms in the house were apportioned to ensure that Debbie had a private space, with the older brothers sharing a room with me. Benny had a small bed in Mom and Dad's room. Johnny and Ronnie shared a bunk bed that was painted a dark shade of yellow-green that Dad had purchased from an army surplus store; I slept in a small bed located in the opposite corner of the room.

In that the house was small, I was in constant physical contact with one or more of my siblings. Debbie was a beautiful sister with long brown hair, brown eyes and a welcoming smile. She often would wear her hair in a ponytail and I delighted in giving it a pull and running away; although she scolded me, she never expressed anger or rage. Johnny and Ronnie looked so much like one another that many people asked if they were twins, even though their ages were two years apart; I always noticed Ronnie's prominent dimples when he would smile. Both my older brothers took great pleasure in playing tricks on me that often resulted in fighting that had to be mediated by our parents. My youngest brother, Benny, was small in stature with a ruddy complexion that accented his red hair and freckles. My older relatives would often tell him how cute he was, making me envious of the attention he was getting.

Our living room was the hub of activity after the dishes had been washed and put away and all chores and homework had been completed. A large sofa and chair, both of which had removable pillows, provided seating for Debbie, Johnny, Mom, and Dad. Ronnie, Benny, and I would lie on the floor, cushioned by the warmth of the large area rug made of soft wool. Sometimes, Benny would sit in Mom's lap, creating additional space for Ronnie and me to stretch out on the floor. When I was in the living room alone during the day, I couldn't resist pulling at the gold, metallic threads that were woven into the fabric covering the sofa cushions; these were the same cushions that my brothers and I would use in pillow fights when both of our parents were away from the house.

A Hoffman black-and-white television in the corner of the living room provided entertainment for our family. On days that I did not attend school, Captain Kangaroo and Mr. Green Jeans captivated me for an hour as I watched while sitting on the floor eating my warm oatmeal or rice puffs cereal. It was a frequent occurrence for someone to have to go outside and move the large antenna around to improve the fuzzy picture on the screen. The antenna provided reception to two television stations - one in Bristol, Tennessee, and the other in Greenville, South Carolina. *What's my Line?* was a family favorite; a local woman, named Betty Lou Stines, who served as a Roane County Coroner, appeared on a segment of the show in 1961. I always looked forward to watching weekend episodes of *The Three Stooges* and *Amos 'n' Andy* with the eyes of our entire family glued to the screen of the television. Benny and I provided no resistance to getting out of bed early on Saturday morning to watch our favorite television line-up including cartoons, *The Little Rascals*, *National Velvet*, and *Sky King*. I especially liked to watch the episodes of *The Little Rascals* in that I got to see colored kids playing, a novel sight for me. When I asked Mom, "Why don't any of the colored kids live in Dawson?" there was a pause and then a reply. "The colored kids live in a coal camp at Coalgap near where your grandparents live," she responded. "I wish they lived close to our house so Benny and I could play with them. That would be a lot of fun," I lamented.

The Hoffman television delivered entertainment into our living room for several years before the picture tube ceased to work. The family turned to radio for its entertainment during the hiatus while Dad saved the money for a new television. WBLR, the local radio station in Harveytown, was on the air from early in the morning until signing off at dusk, always announced by the playing of the national anthem. In addition to the lively music that came over the airways, the "Birthday Club" aired on the station at mid-morning announcing requests that had been received from listeners wishing a happy birthday to their friends or relatives. An announcement of live births at the local hospitals, given by a lady with an enchanting voice, always was proceeded by a lively jingle ending with "...the sweetest little bundle, anyone ever had." In lieu of television viewing time, the family would listen to WABT, a radio station broadcasting out of Wheeler, to follow Virginia State basketball games and the early boxing contests of Cassius Clay, known later as Mohammed Ali. My Dad was our family's boxing enthusiast and always would be excited as each round ended with Cassius getting in his jabs to connect with his opponent.

When our family car, a ten-year-old Ford sedan, became increasingly unreliable, not to mention very crowded for a family of seven, my parents decided it was time for a new car. Dad told Mom that he was going to trade in our old car after he attended a regional Boy Scout meeting in Bristol, Tennessee; that evening he would arrive home in a new car. The entire family was filled with excitement and anticipation at the prospect of getting a shiny new car. "Do you think we might get a red car with lots of shiny metal on it?" I asked my brothers throughout the day. Mom appeared especially excited telling everyone, "When your Dad gets home, I'm going to ask him to take us all for a ride in the new car. We may even go to Mary Lee's Drive-in for ice cream." Her broad smile accented her beautiful blue eyes and ruddy cheeks dotted with a few freckles. She and Debbie corralled us boys for a bath to ensure that we would be befitting of a ride in our shiny new car. At last, Debbie, who had anxiously been watching for Dad's arrival, shouted, "He's home! He's home!" Pushing and shoving to be the first one out the door, Johnny Ronnie, Benny, and I clambered down the front steps. Debbie, displaying her usual demure self, was so excited that she did not protest when she was almost pushed down by her thundering herd of brothers.

Dad proudly called to us, "Come see the new car! I want to show you something special!" He opened the hatch-back door to reveal a large cargo space. "Thomas Lee, you and Benny will get to ride back here," he pronounced. Benny and I quickly climbed in to explore the cavernous area which looked like the perfect club house space for us when the entire family was along for the ride. "Johnny, Ronnie and Debbie will ride in the back seat," Dad told us as the three of them took their places.

The beige Studebaker station wagon, with its wood-paneled sides, seemed massive to my young eyes. The well-upholstered bench seats afforded everyone a place to sit with room left over. The gear shift was located on the steering column behind a substantial steering wheel. The body of the car rested on an elongated frame that gave it the appearance of a funeral hearse absent the curtains draped on the rear windows.

Mom was quick to point out the funeral-like appearance of our car. Consumed with excitement and exploration, I had ignored the conversation Mom and Dad were having by the side of the car. I became more attuned as I heard Mom say, "Tom, I thought you were going to get us a brand-new car. That thing isn't new and it looks like a hearse." Dad's pause revealed his disappointment that Mom was not pleased with the station wagon; he proceeded to try to convince her that the 'woodie' was the perfect car for our family.

Dad had casually mentioned to a physician whom he knew through his professional association with the Boy Scouts that he would be trading in his vehicle for a new one after the scouting gathering had ended. Dad's friend told him that he was interested in selling a used station wagon that he owned and used only as transport to Holston Lake for his fishing expeditions. The vehicle was only a few years old with very low mileage; the body, interior, under-the-hood equipment, and tires all were in excellent condition. Dad's friend was willing to take his car on the trade with Dad paying the difference in cash.

Dad's explanation to Mom that he managed to purchase the car at a cost that was much less than he anticipated spending for a new car seemed to fall on deaf ears. To further persuade Mom, Dad reiterated that the car was almost the equivalent of a brand-new vehicle, easily could accommodate all our family of seven, and had the space with the hatchback door open to accommodate his scouting supplies and equipment. Mom remained recalcitrant, countering with, "You only wanted the station wagon to be able to haul all of your scouting stuff. I am not fooled easily!" Mom acquiesced with time and the vehicle served our family well for several years.

After unusually heavy rains for two or three days, Dawson experienced a devastating flood in 1962. We had made it home safely from Creekside School with Dad pointing out along our way how quickly the water appeared to be rising in the Roane's Fork River. Being pre-occupied with completing a homework assignment in the car, I had not been fully attentive to the conversation and the visible signs of the water elevation in the river until we reached the John's Creek section of Dawson. Peering out the window on the right side of the car, Ronnie shouted, "Look at that! The bottom is completely filled with the water from the river!" Dad noted that he could not remember ever seeing the field covered by that much water and that it appeared severe flooding could occur that night. "Dad, will our house get flooded?" I asked, concerned with my father's sense of alarm. "No," he replied, adding that, "If flood waters reached our home on the hill, every house in the community would be under water." During family dinner, the topic of conversation was the rising water. Mom had relocated the radio from the living room to the kitchen in order to hear WBLR's final newscast before signoff. All ears were attuned to the radio announcer's voice as he provided updated information on the weather, noting that the station would be back on the air later that night if the water continued to rise and flooding was imminent.

My parents' anxiety and concern were palpable throughout the evening as we listened to a radio call-in program broadcast by WABT. As the evening wore on my siblings and I peppered Mom and Dad with questions about flooding, requesting reassurance that no one would be hurt or killed if such an event occurred. Dad periodically moved the knob on the radio frequency of WABT to that of WBLR to check if the local station might have signed back on the air; repeatedly, we only heard static when the dial would be moved to the 1610 frequency. Just as everyone was about to get ready for bed, Dad announced that he would check on WBLR one last time; this time was different in that everyone heard the voice of Ron Potter, owner of the radio station, proclaiming that severe flooding was occurring in the Shacktown section of Harveytown and that residents were being evacuated from their homes in boats by the Roane County Emergency Squad. It became clear that something really bad was occurring and I felt sad. Mom requested everyone to whisper a prayer for those in harm's way as Dad increased the volume on the radio to hear over the static. Mr. Potter was interviewing Howard Franks, Harveytown Water Works manager, who was providing periodic updates on the rising Bigfork River, the confluence of the Roane's Fork, Beetle Fork, and Knob Fork Rivers, and had shared his concern that he had never seen the water level elevate so quickly during all his years of employment at the water plant.

The evening had gotten on and it was now past 11:00 p.m. The radio report indicated that the lower portion of Central Avenue in downtown Harveytown had begun to flood and that evacuation efforts were underway. Mr. Potter continued to plead with Harveytown residents who lived in low-lying areas to evacuate from their homes and seek shelter at one of the centers that had opened to receive them. As my brothers and I scurried off to prepare for bed, I heard Mr. Potter reassure citizens noting, "If the flood waters reach our building, I'll move our equipment on top of the roof, if need be, continue to let you know what is occurring and to advise you of any safety precautions."

I awakened the next morning with Mom telling my brothers and me that there would be no school due to the flooding that had occurred. I felt guilty for being happy that I could stay in bed a little longer knowing that some people were harmed by the flood. We listened to the radio for most of the day, learning even more about the devastation that the flood had left in its path. Citizens were advised to avoid traveling to Harveytown because many of the streets and businesses were still experiencing significant flooding. School continued to be dismissed for the next several days. The front page of the *Harveytown Echo*, our local newspaper, was covered with photographs of the residual effects of the flooding. Windows had been broken in businesses along Main Street and the streets remained covered with a thick coat of mud. The flood continued to dominate our conversation both at home and school for several weeks.

My sister's bedroom always seemed an unpleasant place for me to be; sometimes I was sent there for reflection on my misbehavior. One occasion, I had acquired a bad case of chicken pox and had to be quarantined from Benny in Debbie's bedroom. All other members of the family had experienced the unpleasantness of the virus at an earlier time in their lives. Twisting and turning in the bed, I was extremely uncomfortable due to the uncontrollable itching that the red pustules covering my small body produced. It seemed like new splotches were appearing every minute and that I soon would be red all over like the picture of the clown in my reading book. Mom tried to comfort me by bringing my breakfast to the bed and reassuring me that the itching would not persist for too much longer.

It was almost noon and I remained restless until Mom appeared at the door holding a brown paper bag leaking a liquid that had no doubt originated from its contents. "I brought you a surprise," she proclaimed. Mom opened the bag and removed a plumpish doughnut still dripping with sugary icing. I now could smell the delectable pastry as Mom approached my bed. For a few minutes, I completely was unaware of the itching, focusing instead on savoring the crunchy, sweet taste of the doughnut in my mouth. I hastily consumed the remainder of the treat and requested a second one. Mom left the room to get me a glass of milk to help wash the doughnuts down, after which I rolled over in bed and began to doze.

The ladies at Mom's church had prepared the doughnuts from scratch, along with mouthwatering fried fruit pies, earlier in the day; the pastries were offered for sale to residents of the community as part of the church's fundraising efforts. The pastor at the church spent the day selling fresh pastries going door-to-door to residents in the community. Mom had not participated in the church's endeavor that day in that she had to stay home to care for me.

3/Mom and Dad

Mom's workday started early as she made sure that everyone was out of bed and prepared for school. In addition to serving the breakfast staples of warm oatmeal and puffed cereal, occasionally my mother would serve a special treat of hot, made-from-scratch biscuits along with fried quarters of bologna. I enjoyed this special indulgence best when I halved the hot biscuit and placed the bologna between creating a delicious sandwich. There always were enough biscuits to have a second one teeming with butter and fruit preserves.

Monday was the day Mom set aside to do laundry. The Speed Queen wringer-type washing machine was in the basement of our house as there was no room for it on the main level. Soiled laundry had to be gathered from each of the rooms and taken to the basement; many trips often were necessary to carry all the laundry there.

Clothing items that could not be laundered at home, almost all of which belonged to Mom and Dad, were stored in a small closet in one of the bedrooms to await the arrival of the dry-cleaning man. Mr. Brock drove a small utility van for Hometown Cleaners, located in Harveytown, and covered a route that spanned large parts of the county. Going door-to-door, Mr. Brock would pick up clothing items needing to be dry-cleaned and deliver items already processed.

Once all the clothing had made its way to the basement, Mom would begin the process of treating the water. Our source of potable water was an earthen well that had been core dug by a local drilling company. The water supply was rich in calcium, magnesium, and iron, resulting in hard water and occasional reddish-brown stains on light-colored clothing items if untreated. Although there were cylindrical iron tanks connected to the water supply that filtered out most of the mineral deposits, Mom further treated the water used to launder clothes to better ensure that everything would be devoid of stains.

Building a small fire in a corner of our yard, Mom would place a large, round galvanized tub over the burning logs carrying large buckets of water from a spigot in our basement to be heated in the tub. A small amount of calcium carbide would be added to the water to further break down the minerals; the hot water would then be transported back to the basement to fill the washing machine. This process was laborious and time intensive in that there were several loads of laundry to be done each Monday.

Electric-powered rubber cylinders, or wringer rollers, would compress the clothing to remove as much water as possible after the large agitator in the machine tub and the laundry detergent had done their work. Dirty water from the tub was then pumped from the machine to an underground drain located in the floor of the basement. The entire process had to be repeated for the rinse cycle.

Once the clothes had been washed and rinsed, items would be placed in a large basket and carried outside for drying. Individual clothing items were hung on stretched wire lines and secured with wooden pins containing a metal spring. On windy days, the bedding would be especially difficult to hang. Dad's trousers and Johnny's and Ronnie's blue jeans were stretched on long metal rectangles to assist in eliminating wrinkles in the clothing before being hung to dry. On rainy or snowy Mondays, the washing had to be postponed. Mom never looked forward to washing day as she had to work frantically to complete everything in order to finish in time to prepare dinner for our family.

Tuesday was the time to remove the clothes pins from the laundry hanging outside, bringing it into the house to iron or fold and put away. Mom used a large kettle to prepare a starchy mixture into which select clothing items, such as Dad's dress shirts, would be dipped before ironing. The starch smelled the same as the paste I had used at school to attach pictures cut from old magazines to a sheet of paper. Setting for a time after dipping, items would be unrolled and spread on the ironing board to be pressed. Dad's completed dress shirts would be hung on metal hangers, showing off their smooth, crisp edges. Although the ironing was not as labor-intensive as washing the clothes,

Mom often would announce at the Tuesday dinner table, "My back has been hurting all evening from ironing all day. I'm going to need extra help with cleaning the dishes after dinner." None of the boys was ever in a mood to volunteer to help and Dad would announce whom he had selected to assist Mom and Debbie with the dishes.

In addition to her responsibilities of doing laundry, ironing, and preparing meals, Mom also was tasked as the family's resident seamstress; often during the evening, she would be at her Singer electric sewing machine mending clothing or constructing new clothing items for the family. Mom fashioned most of us boys' button-up shirts in addition to sewing dresses for Debbie and herself. My mother sewed draperies for the windows and on occasion would reupholster furniture. Relatives and friends often sought out Mom to hire her for sewing clothing and other household items.

Mom was charged with managing the family's grocery budget and would shop the Atlantic and Pacific Tea Company (A&P) store in Harveytown every two weeks; since she didn't drive an automobile, Dad would chauffeur her into town on Saturday morning for grocery shopping and to run other errands. Occasionally, Benny and I would be invited to tag along with our parents. Sometimes we would wait in the car with Dad, playing guessing games and watching people busily move about town. If Dad had business to attend to in town, Benny and I would accompany Mom to the grocery store, walking up and down the aisles with our mother as she found the items on her list and placed them in the grocery cart. Staples such as milk, eggs, Velveeta cheese, bread, flour, sugar, cornmeal, butter and oils, potatoes, and canned vegetables always made their way into the cart. Lined writing paper, composition books, and other school supplies had a standing place on the grocery list. Benny and I especially enjoyed Mom's trip to the meat counter where usual purchases included whole chickens, a roll of bologna, ground beef, garlic franks (a special treat for Dad) and an occasional beef or pork roast. Fish portions were found in the cases housing frozen foods and canned salmon was pulled from the grocery shelf. I was especially happy when Mom would choose to buy orange sherbet while shopping the frozen foods case. A special treat was seeing iced spice cake and a box of oatmeal pies selected as our mother moved the cart through the bakery aisle. Multiple packages of Kool-Aid mix in different flavors and a couple of large bottles of ginger-ale were included on the shopping list and were reliably found in the beverage section of the store.

Often Mom would need to stop at the utility offices to pay bills and to visit department stores. I loathed having to visit the clothing stores unless I was being fitted for a new pair of shoes at Levine's Clothing by Miss JoAnn. Miss JoAnn was a pleasant lady who wore a welcoming smile and seemed to have a lot of patience with children running around the shoe department. A new pair of shoes often was accompanied with a flavorful lollipop.

Dad would receive his salary check at the end of the month and it was anticipated by everyone in the family. Of particular interest to my siblings and me were the extra grocery items that were purchased during this monthly shopping trip that would make their way to our Sunday dinner table. As the grocery items were removed from the bags and stored away, I was filled with anticipation of the wonderful feast that would soon be on our table. Mom usually baked and frosted a beautiful cake on Saturday night. The siblings and I would take turns getting a lick off the big spoon of the fluffy, white boiled icing used to top the cake that still contained a few sugar granules that had not liquefied.

On Sunday afternoon after everyone arrived home from church, Mom would quickly and methodically set about to prepare the early afternoon meal. Debbie would assist with peeling and boiling the potatoes and cutting up other vegetables that would make their way into the extra-large ceramic bowl to form the crunchy taste in the potato salad. Mom would simultaneously form the yeast dough for the rolls while assembling the necessary cooking utensils to cut up and fry the chicken. The fresh dough was always covered with a clean dish towel and placed in a warm place to rise. The rolls would be formed by my mother rolling the dough with a wooden pin and then cutting out circles using the top of a beverage glass; each circle would be folded over, brushed with butter, and placed on a baking sheet. Mom would cut up the whole chicken, and then the chicken pieces would be dipped in egg and a seasoned flour mixture before they were placed into a cast-iron skillet of vegetable oil for frying. Mom frequently would add a small amount of bacon grease to the hot vegetable oil if it was readily available. A crisp, brown coating would form on the chicken as it sizzled in the hot oil.

My brothers and I were usually in other rooms of the house or on the front porch as the rolls were baking in the oven. The scrumptious smell of the yeast and flour in the rolls was suspended throughout the house, even making its way through the screened door leading to the front porch. The alluring scent was overwhelming, resulting in a mad dash to the kitchen to beg, "Mom, can we please have a hot roll before dinner? We're really hungry." As soon as the bread was removed from the oven, each of us was given a hot roll with a pat of creamed butter slathered in the middle of the delectable treat. After the entire meal had been prepared, everyone made their way to the table and feasted on fried chicken, warm potato salad, green beans (grown and canned by my maternal grandmother) hot rolls, and a lime green jello salad containing pineapple chunks and miniature marshmallows. I eagerly washed all the food down with a tall glass of Mom's freshly-brewed, astringent iced tea that always was sweetened by the granulated sugar that was stored in a cabinet near the refrigerator. The delicious cake prepared the night before was served for dessert before everyone but Debbie and Mom, who washed and put away the dishes, found a comfortable place to take an afternoon nap.

In spite of her extremely busy schedule, Mom made attendance at church a priority for herself and her family. She was of the Methodist persuasion and Dad attended, albeit infrequently, the Disciples of Christ Christian Church. Saturday nights at our house always included bath time and making preparation to attend Sunday morning church services. The church we attended was down the hill in the lower section of the community, but close enough for us to walk to go there and back. I always looked forward to ascending the long, concrete steps at the front of the church that seemed to go up forever and then jumping back down with my feet landing on every other riser. The church held a youth night service on Wednesday each week and my siblings and I often would attend. It was fun to anticipate the activity where everyone would form a line around the perimeter of the sanctuary, waiting for the sound of the piano, to begin marching and singing a lyrical tune arranged to the "Washington and Lee Swing." When the pianist would abruptly stop playing, everyone would freeze in place; the kid standing closest to the piano at that point and time would be declared winner and receive a cash prize. As I marched anywhere near the piano, an attempt always was made to linger as long as possible, even changing my gait to take small, baby steps, in hopes that the music would stop, and I would be the lucky winner.

Dad's weekday routine during the nine-month school year involved getting out of bed very early in the morning to dress and prepare for school. As seven people shared one indoor bathroom and a single outdoor privy, my father managed to be first in line to commandeer the lavatory to shave. On occasion, I was up early enough to watch Dad run hot water over the wooden shaving brush with soft white bristles, then swirl it into his shaving mug. Dad would apply the lather to his face, making him look like a circus clown. Benny and I would sometimes play with our father's shaving brush, pretending to be all grown up like him.

After putting in a long day of teaching school, Dad usually would remain in his classroom grading students' work and making preparations for the next day. Periodically we would depart from the school as soon as the formal day had ended in order to allow my father to drive into town to borrow media from the board of education office. The Roane County Board of Education administrative offices were in the basement of a building located on Elm Street in downtown Harveytown. Sometimes my brothers and I would be invited to accompany our father to the administrative offices to assist him in carrying supplies and equipment back to the station wagon. Johnny and Ronnie delighted in trying to frighten me by always reminding that the county jail was located on the top level of the building we were entering and that prisoners held at the facility sometimes escaped. Since Creekside School did not have a dedicated library facility, Dad was always excited to borrow books and other visual teaching aids and was especially pleased when one of only a small quantity of the 16-millimeter sound film projectors was available for loan. Dad insisted on carrying the large sound movie projector, telling us boys that it cost a lot of money and he didn't want it to incur any damage on his watch.

In addition to his teaching duties, Dad sponsored a 4-H club for the students attending Creekside School. The club would meet after school had ended and would involve the students learning about and participating in a variety of interesting hobbies. Printed guides and other materials were furnished by the Virginia State Cooperative Extension Service's local agent, who would visit the school program frequently. Woodworking, collecting butterflies, natural resources conservation, sewing, cooking, and public speaking were among the many interests in which students could be involved. Dad's classroom was the largest in the school and housed an electric stove and refrigerator along with a variety of hand tools, work benches, and tables in the rear of the space which got lots of use by club members.

Dad somehow found the time to sponsor and coach a boys' basketball team consisting of students enrolled in 7th grade and 8th grade. Johnny participated as a team member and often would be asked to supervise his brothers after school in creating court boundary lines on the earthen surface using powdered lime that was stored in a large plastic bucket. A trailed line was made by scooping the white powder into a pliable plastic container and letting its contents fall to the ground as one walked a straight line of string that Johnny and Ronnie had placed on the ground. The goals were made with wooden backboards supporting metal rims and were anchored by a large pole that had been cemented into the ground. Other elementary schools in the county would be transported in cars to Creekside School for competitive games.

I was especially excited when Creekside School would play Dawson School at Dawson. We would arrive home early from school on those days and along with Ronnie, I, and sometimes Benny, would walk from our house to Dawson School to watch the game while standing on the sidelines. Sometimes I would manage to slip away from Ronnie's supervision and enjoy the large swings and see-saws located in another section of the school's grounds. At one such game, a player from Creekside School was accosted by an overly-zealous father of a player on the opposing team. Dad quickly intervened, telling the parent, "If you have something to say, say it to me right here." He quickly added, "Don't ever talk to any of my players like that again!" Ronnie observed the confrontation while I was busy enjoying the playground equipment and was delighted to later tell me and the rest of the family that Dad had "...put the man in his place...."

Infrequently when Dad would need to be at Creekside School until late in the evening for meetings, he would arrange for me to ride the school bus home. The only bus that passed by my school and included a route that would eventually take me to Dawson was assigned to Hickory grove School, a small, graded school located close to Dunn Stop School that only served colored children. Dad counseled me the morning that I was to ride the bus, making sure that I knew to board and follow the instructions of the driver without asking questions. I was quite befuddled wondering why it was so important for Dad to take the time to talk with me about riding the bus, repeatedly asking me if I was clear on his directions.

The bus I was to ride arrived at Creekside School and Dad escorted me to its open door, greeting the driver and explaining to him where I would be dropped off. The driver was an amiable man wearing a big smile and a red cap; he welcomed me aboard and directed me to my seat, which was located near the front of the bus. The colored-boy by whom I was seated turned to me, acknowledging my presence, and said, "Hi, do you like going to this school?" I replied, "Yes," and then asked him, "Where do you go to school?" "I go to the Hickory Grove School," he answered. I turned toward the front of the bus as the driver was now back on the road that my Dad traveled when we returned home from school each day. As the bus topped, the big hill beside Bascom Jones' service station, I could now see the large, flashing yellow caution light, a familiar sight that reassured me that we would arrive home soon. However, instead of turning right at the top of the hill to access US 24 south, the driver drove the bus left on US 24 toward Harveytown. Dad had not mentioned that the bus would be going into town, and I became somewhat concerned, turning to my seatmate and asking, "Why is this bus going into town?" He responded, "Oh, the bus always goes into town and on up to Rosenwald High to pick up the high schoolers." He added, "My sister goes to Rosenwald."

I saw lots of familiar stores as the bus made its way through town on to highway 36, making a sharp turn to get to Rosenwald High School. Stopping at the top of the hill, several big kids, who looked to be the ages of Debbie and Johnny, boarded the bus. As my seatmate's sister made her way onto the bus, she stopped at our seat and requested with a wide grin, "May I sit here?" I nodded "Yes" and scooted closer to her brother making room for her to be seated. As the bus began moving again, the teenage girls began to sing a lively song, clapping their hands in unison at the end of each refrain. I was enjoying the joviality and began to clap when everyone else did.

The bus now was traveling on US 24 south and soon arrived at the railroad crossing on the highway just before the turn one would make to go to Coalgap. The driver's turn onto Highway 880 immediately piqued my interest and I became excited that I might get to see my grandparents' house. Instead of traveling all the way to Coalgap, the bus turned right across a wooden bridge and stopped in front of several small houses. Most of the passengers on the bus exited, including my seatmate and his sister.

As the bus traveled on toward Dawson, I silently questioned why the colored kids didn't go to my school or Camden High School. I thought of how I would like to be friends with my seatmate and wondered if he had a tall metal slide and swings at his school. Soon, the bus arrived at the bottom of the hill that led to my house. I made my way off the bus waving goodbye to the kind driver and crossed the highway by John Golden's store, Dawson Market. As I walked toward my house, I couldn't stop wondering why the colored kids didn't go to my school or why I didn't go to their school.

Dad was just as busy at home as he was at school. Our basement was a treasure trove of tools and other fascinating things. There were large tools including a table saw, drill press, planer, and lathe, along with a plethora of hand-held tools such as hammers, screwdrivers, files, vises, drills, and saws. Most of the tools were purchased at an army surplus store, including a massive cabinet that housed every type of screw, nail, drill bit, or utility blade that one might ever need. Dad's paints and varnishes were stored on a large shelf along with sandpaper and balls of steel wool. A variety of smooth lumber was stored in the basement and in the crawlspace area of the house's foundation that was not finished space. The basement floors and cinderblock walls were painted a rich, pine green color similar in hue to the dye in the creosote used to paint the outside of the privy.

Large, white, enamel-coated storage cabinets lined one of the walls of the basement near Mom's washing machine. The cabinets contained an assortment of various and sundry items, not the least of which was a collection of empty cigar boxes that had been saved and given to Dad by Jack Smith and John Golden, local shopkeepers. At the beginning of each school year, Benny and I were allowed to choose one of the boxes in which we could store our pencils, erasers, and glue. A large shower stall occupied one corner of the space that was crafted when Dad and his helpers removed the earth, laid cinderblocks around the perimeter of the walls, and poured a concrete floor with two drains to construct the basement. Mom often told us that the work was especially arduous in that all the cement had to be mixed outside and carried underneath the house to complete the work.

The basement served as a workshop for Dad and a recreation room for all the family. Dad prided himself on crafting several pieces of our household furniture, including bed headboards and footboards, tables, and a small desk; Mom was especially pleased with two beautiful Adirondack lawn chairs my father had made. The outdoor chairs were stored under the crawlspace of our house during the winter and would be taken to the lawn in early spring for a sprucing-up. Benny and I were given small hand scrapers to remove loose pieces of the white enamel paint in preparation for a new coat. Johnny and Ronnie would then sand the chairs before my mother gave them a good washing using the water hose; she sometimes would engage in buffoonery with us boys, pretending that she was losing control of the spray nozzle on the hose and that we all were near certain to be doused with water. With lumber left from making the adult-size lawn chairs, Dad built two smaller ones that fit the bodies of Benny and me like a glove.

My father had purchased a large section of plywood at Harveytown Lumber and Supply in Harveytown and had fashioned a regulation size ping pong table for the family's enjoyment. The tabletop was supported by two wooden sawhorses which previously had been used when Dad and others were working on wood-crafting projects and was located in the center of the room. Benny and I were limited to playing games that ended with one player attaining a score of eleven, while my older siblings and parents played longer matches ending with a score of twenty-one. I always enjoyed watching Mom and Dad play a doubles match against Johnny and Ronnie, faithfully cheering for my parents to win. Mom would become unusually animated and excited, cheering for her team as she maintained focus on being a full participant in the game.

As Benny began to grow, it became a necessity to create space in the house for an additional bedroom. The decision was made to construct a new bedroom on the west side of the house that would serve as my parents' bedroom; Mom and Dad's current bedroom would then be converted to a bedroom that Benny and I would share, providing more space for Johnny and Ronnie. The talk of the project excited the entire family for months before Dad and Eugene Howard, our neighbor and friend, initiated construction by using heavy twine and stakes that would serve as an outline for digging the footers. Eugene's primary job was coal-related, but he occasionally would accept side jobs in construction since he was a skilled carpenter.

Johnny and Ronnie assisted Dad in digging the trenches for the footers and in pouring the concrete base that would serve as the room's foundation. A portable concrete mixer, on loan from a neighbor, was filled with soft sand, cement, and miniature pebbles as water from the garden hose was introduced to create a gray, soupy mush. As the water was added, the power switch would be flipped, and the huge metal barrel would begin to churn. Dad often would check the consistency of the batch to determine whether more water needed to be added. When the mixer had done its work, the power would be turned off and the barrel would be tilted to allow the concrete to be poured into a clean wheel barrow. The wheel barrow would be rolled over to the trenches and be emptied to form the footer; this process was repeated numerous times until all the trench space was filled. Dad and Eugene worked meticulously, guided by level tools that were placed atop the partially solidified concrete that allow more concrete to be added or smoothed away to ensure a flat, level surface around the entire perimeter.

Once the footer was dry, cinder blocks would be laid on which the wooden floor joists would sit. The work could only be done on weekends because both Dad and Eugene had other weekday jobs. I watched with excitement as the walls and the roof were framed and attached to the floor joists, imagining how much fun it would be to have another big room in our house. After a few months, the outside walls, subfloor, and roof were completed, and work commenced on the inside of the space. A large picture window had been created for Mom, who frequently complained that the inside of the house was too dark and needed more natural light. On a late spring day, Dad finally sawed an opening in the existing wall of our house to create an entryway to the new bedroom. Benny and I took turns jumping through the doorway into the new space, excited with new possibilities.

Sheetrock and trim boards were delivered from Harveytown Lumber and Supply and stored in the unfinished room. My brothers and I were tasked with staining all the trim pieces; once the boards were stained, two coats of thin shellac were applied. Dad completed all the additional inside work with the assistance of the entire family. Mom assisted with painting the drywall and ceiling, telling us all that she loved to paint; no one expressed any envy. Precisely cut pine boards formed the finished floor of the room with my father completing all the sanding and shellacking of the finished area.

Dad had planned a special surprise for the room that was unbeknownst to anyone before a delivery of large pine boards arrived one Saturday. A built-in bookcase that Dad had designed on paper began to take form as he measured and sawed the wood to complete the framing and shelves. The finished shelving unit only required that shellac be applied, and my siblings and I helped to complete the work. The unit included a small desk space with a wooden bench crafted to match.

The entire family teemed with excitement as another phase of the project was finished. Mom was ready to have the bed and dresser in her existing bedroom moved into the new space when Dad announced he had another surprise. My parents would travel to Harveytown later that day to shop for a new bedroom suite at Harris Furniture Company. Mom returned home announcing with joy, "Tom bought me a beautiful new bedroom suite that includes a full-size bed, dresser with mirror, chest-of-drawers, and nightstand. I can't wait until it's delivered!" Everyone became excited, quizzing and annoying Mom and Dad about the furniture. Her happiness extended to the entire family.

Once all the furniture had been situated in the room, Dad began to bring boxes of his personal books from school to be placed on the shelving unit. I assisted with taking books from the cardboard boxes used to transport them and would occasionally thumb through the pages of those that piqued my interest. One book in particular, a college textbook on public health, fascinated me with its black-and-white photographs of people who had been afflicted with disease. As I intently stared at a photograph of man stricken with smallpox, I almost became nauseated. The man's entire body, especially his face, completely was covered with pustules and I suddenly imagined that the man's grotesque appearance resembled a hideous monster. I closed the book suddenly, too frightened to continue looking at the photograph. Later, I had to tell my brothers about what I had observed and they, too, had to take a look.

A third surprise from Dad came in a few weeks, when he announced that we would be having a telephone installed. I had observed my Grandma Poe using her telephone and was intrigued by the technology. A phone soon appeared on the desk space of the shelving unit in my parents' bedroom with our assigned number, 304-J, written in the center of the circle of the dialing wheel. Dad explained to everyone that the dialing wheel was not operational, but would be some day, and could then be used to contact and talk with others who had telephones. For now, we would need to lift the receiver and wait until an operator requested, "Number please?" and then tell her the number of the person we wished to contact. Mom announced that Grandma Poe's phone number was 2053-K and that we should call her to better understand how to use the telephone. Mom lifted the receiver and awaited the operator's voice. We all heard her say, "2053-K, please." After a silent pause, Mom said, "I can hear it ringing. Everyone then heard, "Hi, Mama! We got our telephone installed and we're testing it out!"

The telephone became a new-found source of socialization and amusement, as well as annoyance. I told all my friends at school about our telephone and gave them my number. Classmates shared their phone numbers with me, and we regularly called one another, enjoying our conversations. Too frequently, when I lifted the handset to place a call, I would hear others having a conversation. Mom had explained to us that we were sharing a party line with other people and had to be courteous with our use of the telephone. I couldn't help growing impatient when I would try several times to place a call and the same conversation I had heard earlier was continuing.

Often my siblings and I would be overcome with intrigue when we were privy to gripping conversations while checking whether the line was available for a phone call. We would replace the phone receiver after discerning a busy line and then gently pick it up a few minutes later to eavesdrop on the conversation. Sometimes we would be acknowledged with the admonishment, "You hang up that telephone now and stop listening in on us!" If we were caught in the act of listening in on others by Mom or Dad, our privilege to use the telephone would cease for an extended period of time.

My biggest misadventure involving the telephone came one summer when I spent three nights at 4-H camp in Gray, Virginia. Mom was reluctant to let me attend due to my young age, but Dad convinced her that I would be safe and that the experience would be good for me. I overheard my father tell my mother that a telephone was located in the dining hall at the camp that adults could use to call parents if a camper became ill or got injured. When I asked my Dad if I would be allowed to use the phone to call home, he replied, "Absolutely not! The phone is for emergency use only and you don't need to go near it." A local extension agent transported me home from the camp; as soon as I went inside the house, my father called me into his bedroom telling me that my grandmother Brown had told him that she received a telephone call from me while I was at the camp. I was dumbfounded and told my Dad that I had not touched the telephone at the camp. My father proceeded to tell me that I was lying, removing his belt and swatting my behind; the spanking really hurt, but I maintained my innocence. Then I was asked to go into another room and think about my untruthfulness for a time.

I could not imagine why my grandmother would tell my father such an untruth and my crying soon transformed to anger toward her. Dad called me to come back into his bedroom a second time and asked if I now was ready to tell him the truth. I held firm in my innocence prompting more swats with the belt from my father; he continued to attempt to elicit a confession from me which was not forthcoming and after ten or fifteen minutes told me how disappointed he was in me and that I could leave the room. I immediately went to my mother asking if she knew why my grandmother would tell such a lie about me; I got no sympathy from Mom, who told me that she thought I was the one being untruthful. I remained angry with my grandmother for several weeks and refused to visit her house. Finally, my grandmother came to visit me reporting that a child had called her identifying himself as "Thomas" the week I was attending 4-H camp. I snarkily retorted, "Well, it wasn't me. You caused me to get two hard spankings from Dad and I am mad at you." My grandmother began to cry telling me how sorry she was that her conversation with my father had caused me to get spanked, and that she realized that she should have talked with me first about the call before discussing it with my Dad.

I began to search through any books that were in our house. There was no bookmobile service in my community and I was starved for print materials. Through reading, I had discovered that I could venture outside my community, experiencing the circus, the jungle, and towns with lots of tall buildings. We had limited copies of the *Junior Classics* series, *Grimms' Fairy Tales*, and a set of older encyclopedias that had been purchased during bi-monthly shopping trips at the A&P store. I would read for long periods of time when the books were not being used by my brothers and sister; however, I longed for a larger variety of books with captivating pictures, especially those that told stories of travel and adventure.

Dad had brought home many of the sample teachers' editions of elementary textbooks up for consideration for possible adoption by the school district that he was given for serving on selection committees. I would spend hours removing, examining, and reading the large volumes that were assembled on the bookshelves. I especially enjoyed the books that had been considered for adoption as a reading series since I easily could read their stories that were contained in the volumes that corresponded with my grade level. Just to read and explore something different, I would closely examine the preface, table of contents, and authors' qualifications. I wanted to know why the letters Ph.D. or Ed.D. appeared after an author's name or what Teachers' College, Columbia University, had to do with the writer's name.

Dad's involvement in 4-H at Creekside School spilled over to include our entire household and a few other kids in the community. Extra copies of printed materials provided to the school through the local extension office found their way to our house and I devoured them, reading cover to cover. The booklets always contained graphic pencil illustrations to complement the text; most of them were devoted to a particular topic such as creation of a butterfly collection, how to craft something useful from wood, public speaking tips, or home safety concerns. Dad had pulled one such booklet, or *Bulletin* as they were labeled, for me to use to make a wall holder for an ordinary house broom. Dad followed the directions in the bulletin to cut out the two pieces of wood needed for assembly using his table jigsaw, since I was not allowed to use any of the large electric power tools. I was given strips of rough sandpaper and instructed to make all the edges rounded and smooth. Sanding thirty minutes or so without stopping, I would take the wooden pieces to Dad asking, "Have I sanded these enough?" to which he would reply repeatedly, "No, you need to keep sanding until all of the edges are much smoother." I quickly decided that I did not like this woodworking project and would prefer to spend my time reading or playing outdoors. Although I took little pride in the finished broom holder, I could appreciate the beauty of and effort put forth by Johnny and Ronnie in crafting beautiful tables from cherry wood.

Mom would work with Debbie and some of her friends on sewing projects. The girls and my mother would remove large sheets of tissue paper with designs outlined on them from a packet labeled "pattern" along with a picture of the item to be made; they would spread the individual sheets on top of fabric that had been placed on our kitchen table and proceed to place stick pins in the fabric to attach it to the paper. Then they carefully would cut the fabric following the dark black lines printed on the tissue paper. Once all necessary pieces of the fabric had been cut to conform to the patterns, they would begin the process of using Mom's Singer sewing machine to sew the fabric together in accordance with the directions.

Contests would be held at the local, state, and national levels for 4-H club members to demonstrate their skills and talents. Dad had written a speech for me to memorize as part of a local contest on public speaking. I labored for many hours memorizing all the lines. Finally, the Saturday morning that I would give the speech arrived. Dad, Debbie, Johnny, and I were out of bed early, eating a quick breakfast and getting dressed to make the trip to Harveytown. Mom assisted me with my dressing, insisting that I wear clothes that were exclusively reserved for Sunday church. Arriving at the location where the contests would take place, Dad parked the car, and we all made our way into the school building. Along with Dad, I assisted Debbie and Johnny with items they would be using as part of their demonstration speeches.

After we entered the building, Dad escorted me to a large, almost empty, classroom where my debut performance would take place. As Dad was walking to leave the room, I called, "Dad, I'm scared. What if I forget my words?" Assuringly, he responded,

"Don't be afraid. You know your speech and have practiced giving it to me many times. If you forget something, take a big breath, and then go on talking with what you can remember." After a few minutes, two other people came into the room and were seated. One was a teenager who looked to be the same age as my brother Johnny; he was carrying a packet of paper. The other boy was older than I and greeted me with a cheerful "Good Morning!"

Soon, two ladies entered and sat at the back of the room. They introduced themselves as the judges for the speech contest and requested that I give my speech first. I nervously walked to the front of the room and began, "The title of my speech is *Why I'm Proud to Be an American*." I paused for a Moment and then uttered, "When George Washington and his troops first crossed Valley Forge..." before reciting the remainder of what I had memorized and practiced so many times in front of Mom and Dad. I did not forget any of my lines and gained more confidence as I delivered the oratory. At the end of my speech, I returned to my seat with mixed feelings of anxiety, exhilaration, and pride. I listened as the other speakers spoke and wondered why the teenager read his delivery from the papers he held; I hoped he would be disqualified for not having memorized his speech. The other boy had attempted to memorize his speech but became confused shortly after beginning to speak; he was encouraged by one of the judges to begin again which he did. After the third speaker forgot his lines a second time, he just stopped speaking and returned to his seat.

I waited at my seat in the room as Dad had asked me to do as the other two boys and the judges left the room. After one of the judges smiled at me passing by my seat, I couldn't help but think that she had sent me a signal indicating that I had won the contest. In what seemed to be an hour or more, Dad finally came for me. I told Dad that I had not forgotten any lines and may have won the contest. He put his arm around my shoulder while breaking the news to me that I would not be the winner. Dad had run into one of the judges, whom he knew, and she had told him I had done a great job, considering my age, but that I would not be the winner of the speech contest. Later learning that the teenage boy had won the contest, I took solace knowing that I had memorized my speech and he had to be aided by looking at his papers.

Debbie won first place in her demonstration division and received a blue ribbon. The big news of the day was that Johnny not only had won first place in his division, but first place over-all, earning him a trip to Richmond to compete at the state level. Johnny made the trip to the Virginia State Fair with a local extension agent, where he again was awarded first place earning a trip to the National 4-H Congress held in Chicago, Illinois. The next several weeks found our family in a frenzy as we all rallied to support Johnny. Levine's Department Store provided Johnny with a new business suit in recognition of his accomplishment. The county extension agents were abuzz with excitement planning for Johnny's trip to Chicago. We soon learned that Johnny would be accompanied to the event by the local extension agent for 4-H and that both would be staying at the Conrad Hilton Hotel while there. When Johnny returned home, we all were disappointed that he was not a national-level winner but continued to boast to our family and friends of his great accomplishment.

My father's involvement with the Boy Scouts of America had begun in the late 1940s and continued to be his favorite interest. Dad had sponsored an active scouting unit in Dawson for several years, but now was affiliated with a troop that was chartered in Harveytown and held meetings at one of the churches in town. Our basement and crawl space were filled with scouting-related gear. Camping tents were stored in the crawl space area along with several hatchets, long knives, and canteens that were critical to one surviving in the wilderness. Our yard had been home to a large totem pole, spanning ten feet tall and having large wings extending from its body. My father, along with several of his scouting charges, spent countless hours carving a variety of symbols and figures into the large wooden pole that was then painted brilliant primary colors. Dad had to solicit the help of several neighbors to assist in raising and supporting the behemoth-looking creature. The entire family had been schooled by Dad on the importance of the totem pole to the Indian people, who had been constructing them for years and in many instances used them as part of their spiritual rituals; however, Mom was not swayed that the unusual object should remain as part of our lawn, leading to its eventual relocation.

On occasion scouts from Dad's troop would be driven from town by their parents to work on projects at our house on Saturdays. On such occasions, my father would dress in his official scouting uniform that included a dark shirt embellished with colorful, sewn-on patches too numerous to count. A bandana was rolled to display a large triangle before encircling Dad's neck and was held together with a metal clasp. Dad wore a Boy Scouts of America campaign hat with a large felt brim and leather hatband and draw strap reminding me of jungle explorers that I had seen on television. The scouts always would begin their time together by repeating the scouting oath and sometimes taking care of other housekeeping tasks. Sometimes Benny and I were allowed to watch as the scouts worked with colorful plastic beads sewn on leather to make pouches that they would wear as part of their official uniform. Sometimes the boys would sharpen their archery skills by shooting their bows and arrows into a target area my father had temporarily created in our yard.

Before the scouts' parents returned for them in late afternoon, they would enjoy a lunch prepared and eaten outdoors. A fire would be built in our yard in the same location where Mom burned paper refuse, as no solid waste service was available. Once, the scouts made several attempts to ignite two dry twigs, from which the bark had been skinned, by rubbing them together in a rapid motion, hoping for a spark large enough to create fire. Finally, Dad resorted to using kitchen matches to get the fire started. The boys scavenged the yard to locate long sticks that would be sturdy enough to hold a wiener for roasting. Dad would sometimes roast a black-crusted wiener for us boys that tasted delicious after being placed between a Rainbow Bread hotdog roll and topped with mustard and ketchup. After the hotdogs had been eaten, the stick would serve as a handy utensil for roasting large, puffy marshmallows that would melt in one's mouth. Mom would prepare a large pitcher of Kool-Aid that was appreciated by all.

During the summer, the Harveytown troop, along with other scouting troops in the area, would enjoy a week of outdoor adventure at Camp Wilderness. The camp was built in the 1930s, after the land was donated to the Roane County Boy Scouts of America by a local citizen. Several cabins provided lodging for the scouts and a small lake was used for water sports such as swimming and canoeing. The surrounding wilderness provided an abundance of opportunities for the boys to test their acquisition of survival skills. The rugged, mountainous terrain served as home to bounteous and divergent wildlife that could be observed and respected as the scouts hiked the land. Crystal-clear, unpolluted streams of water flowed abundantly in the mountains away from the coal mines and were used for both drinking and cooking. Latrines were prepared by the scouts at the beginning of all camping experiences and located far away from the campsite.

During one summer's week at Camp Wilderness, I had accompanied Dad as the plans were only to stay a couple of nights. Dad and I had been enjoying a pleasant canoe ride on the lake when my father returned to the shoreline with instructions for me to exit from the boat and wait for his return by the earthen dam. After my disembarkment, Dad made his way back out into the middle of the lake to perform a perfunctory task related to the water sports. I decided to sneak down to the shoreline to see if I could spot a fish and accidentally lost my balance and slid into the water. Since I couldn't swim, I quickly went under water; managing to get my head above the water for a Moment, I yelled for my father. He soon rescued me and harshly scolded me for not following his instructions, telling me that I jeopardized my safety; I enjoyed telling everyone about my adventure when the two of us got home.

In addition to his non-compensated leadership role at Camp Wilderness, Dad also spent a month each summer working at a similar camp for scouts in Tennessee. The leadership assignment in Tennessee provided the family with welcomed income during the summer months. Teachers' salaries were paid for nine months during the calendar year, spanning September through May. Mom and Dad had to budget a savings amount from each of the nine months to cover expenses during the summer months when no income was available. Dad's stipend payment from the scouting work during the summer helped fund food and supplies for our family's Fourth-of-July celebration each year along with providing a small cache of money for Mom to save for school clothes and new shoes that would need to be purchased in August.

4/Life in Dawson

Illness and death were aspects of life with which I had limited familiarity. Notwithstanding the occasional respiratory virus, chicken pox, and the mumps, I understood little about chronic sickness or other maladies. Mom had told me that I had a case of measles when I was very young, but I had no memory of it. Cognizant of the need to prevent disease and illness, Mom insisted that my siblings and I be regularly dosed with cod liver oil. The putrid liquid had been recommended to my mother by a doctor in the community and it had regular standing on her grocery list. I would attempt to run and hide when I saw my mother remove the medicinal from the cabinet where it was stored; my older siblings often were called to assist Mom with administering the oil by getting me in a lock hold, forcing my mouth open to accept the spoon of liquid, and then holding my jaws closed to prevent me from spitting the foul-tasting and - smelling substance out. I often would engage in a battle of the wills with my brother, Ronnie, refusing to swallow while he applied unrelenting pressure to my jaw to prevent any expulsion. Sometimes I could fool Ronnie and Mom into thinking that I had swallowed the concoction, only to make a mad dash to the sink to spit it out when the body hold had ended.

Occasional scrapes and bruises were treated with mercurochrome, an orange-colored liquid that burned like accidentally touching the big stove in the living room during the winter. While trying to learn to ride my blue bike with training wheels, I inadvertently ran the tires over a large pebble causing the bike to tilt and eventually topple over. As the bike went down, so did I, tearing the skin off my elbow and knee. I managed to pick the bike up off the street and make my way home, sobbing for the entire journey. Mom was working in our yard and heard the commotion. After meeting me at the gate and consoling me, she disappeared briefly into the house to get the mercurochrome. When my mother returned and the dreaded orange medicine was spotted, I turned up the volume of my sobbing shouting, "No! No!

Please Mom! Don't pour the orange medicine on me. It will burn really bad!" Trying diplomacy, Mom advised me that the medicine would kill all the germs and help the pain to go away; when that failed, she told me if I didn't allow her to put the medicine on my elbow and knee that she would have to take me to the doctor and let him do it. Summoning as much courage as I could muster, I held my breath while the orange medicine trickled over first my elbow and then my knee. As anticipated, the medicine did burn, with the pain I felt being somewhat mitigated by Mom rubbing my back and singing to me.

Local physicians, Dr. Smith and Dr. Taylor, had small offices located near Dawson. I had visited their offices once or twice to receive stitches for a small injury and to get a shot for some purpose. Both physicians made house calls, always carrying their brimming black satchels. I received my immunizations for school at the health department office located in Harveytown. I was coaxed into going with the promise of getting a toy at the A&P store afterwards. A nurse with a commanding presence, Mrs. Rickett, poked the needle into my arm causing me to scream "Ouch! That hurt!" that Mom said could be heard throughout the office building.

The polio vaccine was administered in a small sugar cube that was distributed to the entire Dawson community on a Sunday afternoon at the Dawson School. A long line had formed when we arrived, and it took us an hour or more to make our way to the tables where the sugar cubes with the medicine dotted on top were passed to those waiting. The polio vaccine dosing tasted far better than the spoonful of cod liver oil that I was forced to take on a regular basis, and it was certainly more pleasant than Mrs. Rickett's needle.

One afternoon, Ronnie and I were taking turns swinging with our arms stretched on metal posts that supported Mom's clothes lines. There were two posts in the ground, one on each end of the yard, with a second, wide post attached to each top. The wide posts at the top were perfect for gripping with both hands, raising our feet off the ground, and swinging. It was Ronnie's turn, and he was wearing a wide grin as he propelled his body back and forth. Without warning he fell to the ground shouting, "My arm is hurt! Please go get Mom!" Hearing our shouts, both Mom and Dad ran toward Ronnie and coaxed him to roll over so they could examine his arm. Dad noticed that Ronnie's arm had begun swelling and asked Mom to bring some ice. Ice was applied but the swelling did not dissipate. Moreover, Ronnie continued with the sobbing pleas for help. After a brief discussion, it was decided that my brother needed to go to the hospital to determine if the bone in his arm was broken. Dad and Mom transported Ronnie to the hospital where an X-ray indicated that he had broken his ulna bone. My brother returned home wearing a white cast on his arm, but relieved of the intense pain and discomfort he was experiencing earlier.

The first time I experienced death first-hand was when a little girl, who appeared to be younger than I, passed away. Her family lived a few houses up the street from our house and I had only seen the girl on occasion playing in her yard. Mom was crying as she told Benny and me that the little girl had a type of cancer called leukemia and that she couldn't get well and had gone to Heaven to be an angel. I decided that I didn't want to be an angel anytime soon and quizzed my mother regarding my possible demise. Mom, as always, was comforting and reassuring, telling me that I most likely would not die and become an angel until I grew to be very old.

A very old woman, whose grandchildren I knew from our church, was critically ill and Mom wanted to pay the family a visit. Mom was acquainted with the lady and her family and remarked, "I've always liked Mrs. Spicer and I am so sorry that she is so sick. I feel like I must go and see her before she passes on." Mom told me that I would need to accompany her on the visit because I was too young to be home alone unsupervised. As we walked up the street toward the house where Mrs. Spicer was being cared for, Mom told me that I needed to be very quiet during the visit inside the house and to not become restless or fidgety. Mom held my hand as we entered the room where Mrs. Spicer appeared to be sleeping in her bed. Mrs. Spicer's mother-in-law accompanied us and told Mom that the doctor had advised them that death could happen at any time. I was happy to see that Mrs. Spicer was not crying or hurting since she was so sick. Mom held Mrs. Spicer's hand for a few minutes, and we returned home.

A few days after our visit, Mrs. Spicer died. I was in the yard with Mom when we both saw a black hearse traveling toward her house. Mom told me that the letters in the back window of the hearse read Harveytown Funeral Home, which was owned and operated by the Dawson family, and that she was almost certain that Mrs. Spicer had died, as we later learned had been the case. Mom made preparation to attend the funeral service for Mrs. Spicer to be held at the Methodist Church. For some strange reason, I decided that I would like to attend the funeral. I asked Mom if I could go, and she told me that it probably would not be a good idea. My curiosity had been aroused concerning all things death and I persisted in nagging my mother, begging to attend the funeral service. Mom attempted to dissuade me by likening my attendance at the funeral with things I viewed as unpleasant such as church behavior. I would have to wear my Sunday clothes, sit still, and be quiet for an extended period of time. I was unrelenting, and my mother finally conceded.

We walked to the church, which wasn't very far from our house. Upon arriving, I noticed the black hearse parked in front of the building. Mom and I entered the church and found a full room with only a few seats remaining in the long, wooden pews. We took our seats on the end of one of the pews shortly before the service was to begin. A large metal cabinet, turned on its side and resting on a frame with wheels, was in the front of the church with beautifully arranged flowers on its top. Mom told me that the big object I thought to be a cabinet was a casket, and that Mrs. Spicer's body was inside. My mother had whispered, "When the service is over, the undertakers will open the casket and you will be able to see her body." Throughout the service, I could not stop thinking about how a dead person would feel to the touch. "Would the body feel like my body or my Mom's body?" I speculated. I continued my rumination, finally turning to Mom with a whisper, "Can I touch Mrs. Spicer when they open the casket she is in?" "Absolutely not!" Mom hastily whispered. "Be quiet and pay attention to the service," she added. When the service had ended, men dressed in dark suits made their way to the front of the church and began to roll the casket down the aisle toward the rear of the building. The men then returned to the front of the church and began directing all the people seated in the pews out of the building. A line had formed in the aisle, and it was a long wait before Mom and I were motioned to now join the line. As the people in front of my mother and me moved out of the church, I caught a glimpse of Mrs. Spicer's body lying in the casket lined with silk; she was dressed in her nightgown and didn't look much different from when I had seen her a few days earlier in her bedroom. As I drew closer and closer to the casket, I felt a burgeoning internal struggle. "Should I go ahead and touch Mrs. Spicer to learn how a dead person feels and hope that Mom won't be too angry with me, or should I obey my mother?" I pondered. My youthful impetuousness took control, and I placed my fingers on Mrs. Spicer's arm. My mother quickly pulled my arm away and held my hand tightly until we had exited the building. Once outside the church and no longer within earshot of anyone else, I received a stern rebuke that I would not soon forget.

My siblings and I were never happier than when we were all playing games together. One of my favorite pastimes was to share our front porch with my sister and brothers. The older kids would usually get the coveted seats in the bench swing while everyone else sat on the floor or the steps leading up to the porch. We could spend hours playing a game that involved guessing the color, type, or model of the next vehicle that would appear on the street with each one of us keeping track of correct guesses; the first one to reach ten correct guesses would be declared the winner.

"Hide and seek" was a game in which everyone could participate and was usually played at dusk when it was easier to remain hidden from the designated hunter. Some of Mom's younger sisters, who were close to us in age, were visiting with my Grandma Poe when Ronnie suggested that we play "hide and seek" in our basement. All the kids bounded out of the house and into the basement while Mom and our grandmother remained upstairs to drink coffee and chat. Someone suggested that we make the game scarier by calling the hunter "Larry," after a man whom we knew who could frequently be seen walking around the community. We had enigmatized the man, not understanding why he did not speak or appear to hear. After a few rounds of the game, it was my turn to assume the role of "Larry." I positioned myself near the large, double wooden door at the front of the basement, closed my eyes, and began counting to one hundred while everyone else hurriedly ran about the room looking for a hiding place. After I had finished counting, I heard a faint noise that seemed to be coming from outside the doors. I slowly opened the doors and was dumbfounded and terrorized simultaneously. Larry was standing near the door and was smiling at me! I froze and after gaining my composure, I hurriedly closed the door without uttering a word. I made my way back to the rear of the room and softly announced that everyone should come out of hiding since I would not be hunting them. I went on to say that I was very scared and that someone needed to go get my mother. For the longest time, no one would come out of hiding thinking I was playing some sort of trick just to be able to tag them and announce, "You're Out!" When I sat in the floor for a time hanging my head and remaining silent, Debbie finally appeared and asked what was wrong. I told her that Larry was standing outside the door and that I had seen him after hearing a noise and opening the door. Debbie, knowing where everyone else was hiding, rounded them up and told them what I had said. We all decided that we should go together to open the door in case the man was still outside the doors. Everyone cautiously moved together toward the doors with Ronnie leading. He opened the door quickly and announced that no one was there and that I had lied to everyone. I continued to implore everyone to believe me even venturing outside by myself to search for the elusive Larry. Looking up and down the street and all around the outside of the house, there was no sign of anyone in sight. Everyone resumed playing in the basement except me. I frantically went into the house to tell Mom and my grandmother what had occurred, hoping that Larry would come back and scare Ronnie.

Benny and I would delight in gathering our toy cars and trucks and finding a place on the dirt floor under the crawl space section of house to play. Mimicking the large trucks loaded with coal that we would observe on the highway that ran in front of our house, we could spend hours at a time grading roads in the dirt using a toy scraper truck. Bridges would be constructed out of scrap wood and our larger toy trucks and the scraper would be used to haul loads of coal to a pretend dump site. Our cars and trucks would be positioned to move about the roads with us deciding that we needed an occasional collision to keep the activity exciting. The cars would be smashed into one another with one being overturned and sitting on its top. A toy ambulance in another section of the space, positioned far away from the crash site, would then be summoned. I often would navigate the ambulance on the road while vocalizing shrill pitches with my voice that resembled the sirens that we had heard while watching television programs. When the ambulance had made its way to the collision site, we would pretend to put people into the vehicle to be transported to the hospital.

When large snows would come and school was dismissed, I would excitedly join my siblings and other kids in the immediate neighborhood to go sledding down the street beside our house. The street featured an incline of about twenty-five degrees and was flanked by a large ditch on the side opposite our house. My siblings and I would get dressed in warm winter coats and gloves before going outside the house. Mom would insist everyone to wear a wool toboggan that was to remain pulled down over our ears. Every so often someone would have lost or misplaced a glove and would have their hand fitted with two cotton socks, one layered on top of the other. Our family owned one sled that everyone had to share.

As we made our way to the top of the hill, everyone would be careful to only walk on the sides of the street to not risk any damage to what would become our snow slope for the next few hours. Johnny and Ronnie would be first to take turns riding the sled down the hill to compact the powdery white snow and to make certain that there were no moguls that could interfere with the sleigh's rapid descent. When the snow cover was particularly deep, one of my brothers would have to pull the other one seated on the sled down the hill using the large rope that was attached in order to create runner tracks.

The sledding fun usually began with each one having a turn to ride the sled solo down the hill. As the packed snow track became slicker and faster, my siblings and I would layer two, and sometimes three, passengers on the sled to make the exhilarating trip down the hill. Everyone laughed uncontrollably when the sled would veer from the established track and crash into the ditch. When some of the neighbor kids would come out to join the fun, the snow track would be extended to the top of the Howard family's driveway adding at least fifty yards to its length. To allow everyone to use the snow track more quickly, the search was on to locate empty cardboard boxes that could be torn apart to create a make-do sled; if the cardboard was waxed on one side, the velocity of the ride down the hill increased. Larger cardboard pieces could accommodate four or more passengers and allow for sitting rather than lying on its surface. Everyone would be delirious when several passengers sledding down the hill on a cardboard surface would crash, causing its passengers to topple over one another.

Heavy snows with significant accumulation would give cause for us kids to work together to construct an igloo in our yard. Balls of snow would have to be rolled to increase in size just as if a giant snowman was being formed. The gigantic snowballs would be placed side-by-side and on top of each other before being packed down by several hands working in tandem. Once the structure had the appearance of one enormous snowball, the process of tunneling inside would begin. My fingers, along with those of my siblings, would be transformed into squirrels' claws, chiseling away at the mammoth structure and being careful to always pat and pack the remaining structure as the work was completed. It took several hours to finish the work and we often would require a trip to the privy, then to the house for washing our hands and warming our bodies. The finished igloo made a cozy clubhouse for three or four kids to crawl into at one time.

Halloween in the neighborhood was a special time of year, eagerly anticipated by young and old alike. Face masks lined the racks and shelves of the A&P store during this time of year, along with large bags of suckers, bubblegum, and candy. Costumery fell to the mothers of the community and often showcased unusual creativity. Mom utilized old clothing items and other dry goods to help everyone in our family create unique costumes. My personal favorite, which I chose to wear for consecutive Halloweens, was a ghost costume that Mom made from an old white sheet. Old paper grocery bags or old pillowslips were used to carry the treats that we would receive while visiting our neighbors' houses.

One Halloween found me late in getting my costume on and making my way out of the house. It already had begun to get dark outdoors and trick-or-treaters were out making their rounds. Hearing a knock at the door, I took the bowl of treats that were to be distributed and opened it slowly. Three older kids, all dressed in costumes, collectively said, "Trick or treat!" As I began to place treats in the bags, my eyes were drawn to the kid in the back who was colored, an exact resemblance of the kids with whom I had ridden on the school bus months earlier. I called out, "Mom, come to the door to see the trick-or-treaters." My mother made her way to the door and did not offer a smile and her usual pleasant greeting to the kids, instead telling me, "You need to close the door." I asked Mom if the colored kid lived in Dawson and she answered, "No. And that was not a colored boy. He should be ashamed of himself for disrespecting colored people." I was befuddled and asked my Mom to explain why she said the kid was not a colored boy; Mom explained to me that the kid who looked like a colored boy had collected black soot from a stove pipe and mixed it with Crisco shortening to create a black paste which he had used to cover his face, arms and hands. She continued her rant that his costume was shameful and that his mother should not have allowed him "...to get out in public looking like that."

Benny and I always were accompanied by Debbie during the trick-or-treating activity because of Mom's concern with our safety. Everyone often was reminded by our mother that, "...some people do really mean things on Halloween. Our neighbors have had their privies overturned and some older boys set old tire casings on fire in the middle of the road...."

Most of my neighbors placed a colorful sucker in my bag while others gave me a Tootsie Roll or a piece of Kitts candy. One neighbor treated me with a home-made popcorn ball that had a delicious coating of sugar and corn syrup. My absolute favorite place to go on Halloween was to Mr. Petrelli's house, located several blocks out the street from Smith's Grocery. It was a tiring walk and there always was a long line of kids waiting for a special treat. Mr. Petrelli would drop a full-size candy bar into my treat bag for me to enjoy. I didn't get to enjoy this confection too often without having to share with a sibling.

As Debbie and I were walking down the street after several house stops had been completed, I remarked, "My treat bag is getting really heavy to carry. I can't wait to get home to eat them." Unbeknownst to the two of us, an older boy was stealthily approaching us. Without warning, I felt my treat bag being snatched away and saw the shadow of an older teenage boy running away from us, carrying my treats. I began to cry while Debbie yelled at the boy, "You come back here with that treat bag! You snatched it from my brother, and he is just a little kid!" When the boy continued running and it became obvious that he had no intention of returning my treat bag, Debbie again yelled, "You should be ashamed of yourself for taking a little kid's treats. Why don't you try doing that to someone your own size? If you eat my brother's treats, I hope you get sick and throw up!" Debbie then turned to me and gave me a hug, saying that she was sorry about what had happened and that I would still get to eat candy because she would share some of hers with me. "I am tired and mad and just want to go home," I told Debbie. My sister agreed that it would be best if we went home.

Debbie and I turned toward our house at the next street corner and began walking at a brisker pace, passing several other kids along the way. I continued to pity myself that I would not be returning home with a bag full of delicious treats like the other kids we encountered. Adding to my misery, I suddenly tripped and fell, planting my hand on a sharp, piercing object. Debbie managed to get me to my feet and examined me to discover that I had small puncture wounds in my hands that were beginning to ooze blood. Alarmed she exclaimed, "What happened? What did you fall on? Was it a broken soda bottle?" I sobbed that I didn't know. Looking at the street pavement in front of us, my sister picked up a piece of shiny metal shouting, "This is barbed wire! Someone put this on the street, and you fell and hurt your hands on it. Why would anyone do this? We've got to hurry home really fast."

My tears continued until we arrived home due to the stinging pain in my hands. Debbie agitatedly explained to Mom what had happened, and my mother went straight to the medicine cabinet where the Mercurochrome was stored. My crying intensified as she led me to the lavatory in the bathroom to run water over my wounds to remove any dirt or debris before dousing both hands with the orange medicine. Since my hands already were stinging from the pierced skin, the medicine didn't seem to heighten my discomfort. Once my composure had somewhat returned, Debbie brought me several pieces of candy to enjoy. Although the small pieces of candy placated me to a certain extent, I remained sad that I had been denied the pleasure of sinking my teeth into the much-anticipated candy bar given to me earlier by Mr. Petrelli. I, too, hoped the mean boy, who stole it, would get sick and throw up.

5/Neighbors

The Youngs were neighbors who lived directly across the street from our house. Mr. Young, who served as minister of the Baptist church, taught at a graded school for a few years on a temporary certificate before returning to college to earn his bachelor's degree. Mrs. Young managed all the household chores in addition to her work as a secretary in the internal medicine department at Harveytown Hospital. The Youngs had a son, Chad, who was my favorite playmate. Chad was several years younger than I and Mom cared for him in our home while Mrs. Young was at work. Chad was an affable boy whom my Mom loved like a son; he was often included in our family's activities and was allowed to occasionally spend the night with Benny and me; at times during sleep overs, Mom or Debbie would prepare popcorn for us in a large kettle on the stove, letting us watch and listen as the kernels popped open. Chad enjoyed playing cars and trucks with Benny and me and sometimes would bring items that he had found in his basement that could be used as pretend culverts as part of the labyrinth of roads and bridges that Benny and I had designed.

Benny and I always looked forward to being invited to spend the night with Chad. The three of us would sleep in his large bed and enjoy our time of reading stories from *Grimms' Fairy Tales* and other children's books that were shelved in a small cabinet in his room. Chad's Mom would make hot cocoa topped with miniature marshmallows for everyone to enjoy before bedtime; sometimes the beverage was served with a delicious chocolate-chip cookie. Chad's mother would come into his bedroom just before the lights were turned off to lead us in our night-time prayers. I always felt snug and secure while falling asleep in Chad's bed.

Benny and I had coaxed Chad into asking his Dad to consider making a clubhouse for us in a wooded section below the Youngs' yard. The spot we had selected was not maintained as part of the lawn but was part of the lot's acreage. Not only did

Chad's father agree to build us the club house, he met with us to plan all the details. The shack was framed from two by fours and other scrap lumber that Chad's Dad had in his garage. Used sheets of slate that had been discarded by the school where Mr. Young formerly worked formed the roof for the structure. Benny and I were able to purchase inexpensive plastic that was packaged as a covering to winterize glass-paned windows to cover the sides of the structure. We boys particularly enjoyed being in the club house during a hard rain, listening to the droplets of water pinging on the slate roof. I enjoyed eating snacks and telling scary stories in the structure and sometimes would lie down and take a quick nap.

The Howard boys, Robert and Jimmy, lived up the street and would frequently invite us to their house to play. The Howards' yard backed up to the slope of the mountain and never lost its appeal for exploration. In the summer of the year, large green grasses that had been allowed to grow without disturbance covered the hillside. The grasses would turn brown in the fall with a shiny brown coating appearing on each of the tall blades. Robert had conjectured that if the grass was trampled down, it would make a slick surface for riding the pieces of cardboard just as we used as a sled in the snow. We used several pieces of our scrap cardboard just to flatten a run down the hillside. Trial and error informed everyone that the best results were achieved using the cardboard with the waxed surface on the bottom. "Sled rides" on the cardboard from the top of the hill lasted longer and were faster than the snow runs we had used on our street. None of us could contain our excitement when everyone would board the cardboard and experience the fun of a tumbling crash half-way down the slope.

John Nolan was a neighbor who lived a few blocks away from our house. Mr. Nolan worked as a coal miner during the day and would often arrive home in his bank clothes (mining attire) and a metal hat with a light attached to the front. Benny and I often would be directed by our mother to position ourselves in the yard to watch for Mr. Nolan's vehicle to make its way up our street after he had finished his work shift. The two of us would walk to Mr. Nolan's house to ask if he was available to give us a haircut. The gentleman was a kind-hearted, accommodating man who never declined our request; he usually would ask us to wait in his basement for him while he took some of his mining supplies into his house. He had acquired a tall chair in which he would ask his customers to sit while he cut their hair. A large, bright light bulb was suspended from the ceiling on a long electrical cord. The power clippers would be connected to a plug adapter that was screwed into the socket housing the light bulb. The clippers would move over my head, and I would feel the hair fall on my shoulders and back. Wearing thick glasses, Mr. Nolan often would say, "Be still, son. I don't want to gap you." When the cut was complete, I would stand reaching into the pocket of my pants to find the quarter to pay. Remembering Mom's instruction, I always remembered to thank Mr. Nolan before returning home.

Across the street on the west side of our house was Millie and Noble Caton's property; it was marked off with a tall fence that spanned the perimeter of the acreage. Both Mr. and Mrs. Caton were up in years, yet they remained active by working in their flower and vegetable gardens. Mr. Caton tended a large vegetable garden located in the lower section of his lot. Tall rows of sweet corn, along with several rows of bushy tomatoes, potatoes, squash, and cucumbers could be seen from our street during the summer months. Mr. Caton could be observed from the large window in Mom's and Dad's bedroom working in his garden for hours at a time, always wearing a button-up shirt, baggy trousers, and a straw hat with a wide brim. My entire family looked forward some of the fresh tomatoes that Mr. Caton would share when he would harvest his crop each year. Mom would visit with Mrs. Caton frequently, often spending several hours conversing while admiring her beautiful flowers that were dispersed all around the yard. Mom told everyone that the secret to Mrs. Caton's beautiful summer blooms was the snuff-laden spittle that was yielded from the plug of the tobacco that she would hold under her lower lip.

Directly across the highway from our front porch, Raymond Tolliver would sit for hours in his rocking chair and listen to professional baseball games on his radio. I would always wave to him and say, "Hello!" when I would see him. Mr. Tolliver was an elderly man who lived with his wife, Faye; he retired early from mining coal due to a lung ailment. The Tolliver's children were grown and had moved away from Dawson to find employment. I observed Faye spending most of her time working, always wearing a crisply ironed, white apron. Mom had visited in the Tolliver's home and had told my siblings and me that the house was immaculate, with "...everything in its place and the floors clean enough to serve as dinner plates." The Tolliver's lot was accentuated with a finely-manicured privet hedge line with several large trees growing in the yard. I had watched from our front porch as swarms of bees would go in and out of a large hive secured high in a branch at the top of one of the trees.

While playing in my yard one morning, I observed as a large truck park in the Tolliver's driveway. Several men got out of the vehicle dressed in strange-looking suits that had hats that were sown to the top with a net in the front. Mr. Tolliver came into the yard to talk to the men while watching them climb a ladder to the top of the tree where the hive was located; fanning a bellows that emitted a dark smoke toward the hive, the men watched as a large swarm of bees exited their dwelling. Many of the bees lit on the suits of the men, frightening me that they would be stung over and over. Johnny, who knew more than I about what was taking place, assured me that the men would not be stung due to their suits being made of a thick fabric. An hour or so later, most of the bees had left the giant hive and flown elsewhere. The men took a long pole and knocked the hive out of the tree branch that was holding it before slicing it open with a giant utility knife. The opened hive exposed what looked to be a large waxy structure with lots of identically-shaped, small holes; Mr. Tolliver examined the structure closely while the men transferred it to a large plastic tub in the back of the truck. My older brothers told me that sweet, dripping honey, just like what we spooned from a jar to put between a biscuit, would be rendered from the big object the men had put in the tub.

One morning I awakened with a headache, upset stomach, and nausea. It was decided by my parents that I should not attend school until I had recovered from whatever malady had befallen me. After getting out of bed and going to the bathroom, I returned to my bed burrowing myself under the warm, comforting quilts. After an hour or so, Mom came to check on me and ask how I was feeling. I told her that my head continued to ache, but my stomach was beginning to settle. Mom told me that she would be visiting with one of the neighbors for a short while and that I should remain in the bed and not be stirring around the house. My mother reminded me of a conversation between Dad and her last evening to which I was privy regarding a neighbor who was AWOL from the armed services and hiding out in his parents' home. As Mom left my bedroom, she reiterated, "Don't get out of your bed. I will be back shortly. The military police may be around here looking for that man." I rolled over and tried to return to sleep, to no avail. I could not stop thinking about the man who was in trouble and the police looking for him. My mind ruminated incessantly, "What if that man breaks into our house trying to keep from getting caught? What if the police see him come into our house and follow him inside? What if the police decide to shoot him?" I burrowed myself even deeper into the bed in a state of panic, hoping that my mother would be home soon to protect me. It seemed like hours that I waited for Mom's return. When she returned forty-five minutes or so later and called for me, I was too terrified to even answer; she quickly came into my bedroom pulling back the quilt and asking, "Why didn't you answer me when I called?" I burst into tears and told her that I was too afraid to answer because I thought the hunted man and the police might be in our house. Mom profusely apologized to me for being gone longer than she had expected and for even going at all.

The Jacobs family lived a few houses up the road from my house. The older girls, Lana and Susan, were close friends of my sister and would come to our home for visits. On occasion, Mom would let the girls use her sewing machine to construct or repair clothing. Ronnie and I were friends with the teenage girls' brother, Wade, who was closer to us in age. Occasionally, we would walk to and from church with Wade and his siblings.

Dad had assembled a small bow for Ronnie and me to shoot arrows into a large target with colorful concentric circles. Ronnie, Benny, and I often had watched boys from Dad's scouting troop shoot their bows and arrows during Saturday outings and begged our father to let us try the sport. Dad was adamant that we only used the bow in our own yard and were to only shoot at the designated target. Most of the boys of my age, who lived in Dawson, had watched westerns on television and were very much aware that brave Indians could skillfully use a bow and arrow as their primary weapon while engaging in a battle. Frequently, Benny and I would play the game of cowboys and Indians with our friends; half of the boys were assigned the role of cowboy, with the others pretending to be Indians. The cowboys would wear toy holsters that held shiny metal toy guns that could make a loud noise when caps were fired; several rolls of red caps, paper with dots that contained a small amount of gunpowder that made a loud pop and emitted smoke from the toy gun, were included with the purchase. Boys assuming the role of Indian would carry toy bows with a quiver of arrows, each of which had a large rubber suction cup on the end designed to prevent injury. A pretend battle would ensue with weapons being drawn and used to take down the enemy.

I had told our friend, Wade, about our bow and bragged about how much fun it was to shoot the arrows into the target. Wade had invited Ronnie and me to his yard for a visit and requested that we bring the bow and arrow along. Despite knowing that we were restricted from leaving our yard with the bow and arrow, caution was thrown to the wind, and we headed to Wade's house to play. The three of us spent perhaps an hour taking target practice in the Jacobs' garden plot, which was dormant in the late fall of the year. As Ronnie and I were about to exit the yard, we noticed two large buckets that were hanging on the side of the garage. Wade explained to us that the buckets served as slop containers and that their contents, food scraps that remained after his family had their meals, would be taken to a farmer who raised hogs. Ronnie turned over in his mind what might happen if we shot one of the arrows into the side of the bucket, and then shared his thought with Wade and me. Wade asked, "Do you want to find out? Ronnie, go ahead and shoot it." Expressing his reticence to do so Ronnie replied, "If I do it, you'll have to do it too, so I'm not the only one in trouble." The suspense built as Ronnie pulled the bow back and released, sending the arrow into the slop bucket. When I pulled the arrow out of the bucket, a steady stream of liquid began to flow. Laughing aloud, I exclaimed, "Look! The slop bucket is pissing!" The other two boys joined me in laughing and Wade took his turn at shooting not one, but two or three arrows into the bucket. As expected, liquid streams flowed from all the holes in the bucket when the arrows were removed adding to our uncontrollable laughter and hilarity. When I caught a glimpse of Mr. Jacobs, eyeing his son Wade who still had the bow in his hands, I knew the three of us were in a world of trouble. Looking directly at Wade, Mr. Jacobs asked, "Did you do this?" With his head bowed, Wade nodded, "Yes," without adding that the Brown boys had been involved as well. Mr. Jacobs removed his belt and proceeded to give Wade a correction that would not soon be forgotten. Turning to address Ronnie and me, Mr. Jacobs said sternly, "It's time you boys got on home, and don't bring that thing back up here." As I walked home, I felt really bad for Wade and guilty that Ronnie and I had escaped a well-deserved punishment.

Unless inclement weather was at hand, we could observe the activities of our neighbors as we sat on our front porch. Many of our neighbors did not own automobiles and were reliant on a single public transit source that served communities throughout Roane County. The SVTC (Southwest Virginia Transportation Company) bus lines operated large red and black coaches that ran hourly routes on Highway 24 between Harveytown and Dawson; the bus allowed local citizens access to larger grocery stores, such as the A&P chain, that carried a larger selection of foods and a variety of other items than what could be stocked by the neighborhood grocers. It was not unusual to see several family members walking on the side of the road carrying large paper bags of groceries after arriving back to the Dawson bus stop from a shopping trip to Harveytown. Sometimes an unfamiliar man or woman would stop at our house, handing the family member who answered the door a note that told of a dire family circumstance and requesting food. Everyone had been instructed by our mother to always be kind to the beggars and to give them a couple of cans of food that was stored in the pantry shelf. With the exception of a very limited food commodities distribution program, federally- or state-funded nutrition assistance programs were mostly non-existent. When I was our family's recipient of a beggar's note, I always had feelings of confusion and sadness after the solicitor had left our door. It was perplexing for my young mind to fathom how one could not have any food to eat when there always was a lot of food on the shelves at the A&P.

Some of our neighbors were entrepreneurs, selling their wares by going door-to-door in the neighborhood. One man had sold our family an Electrolux vacuum sweeper that had fascinated me as a toddler with its pipes and hose. Mrs. Napier, who lived several miles east of our house, kept chickens and would sell fresh hen eggs to the neighbors by walking door-to-door; she was an old woman who wore a sun bonnet and a long dress. The skin on her face was wrinkled, thick, and leathery, and she reminded me of a picture in a school story book of the mean old lady who hurt boys and girls. After purchasing some of the eggs, Mom told Benny and me that Mrs. Napier had told her that she had little money and used what she collected from the sale of her eggs to buy food. Sensitive to Mrs. Napier's plight but remaining frightened of her and anything associated with her, we boys announced, "Don't prepare any of those eggs for us. We won't eat them!" Mom surreptitiously removed some of the eggs in the paper carton from the A&P store and replaced them with eggs purchased from Mrs. Napier. A day or so later, I requested Mom to make fried eggs for us to eat for breakfast with the admonition, "You better use the eggs in the A&P carton and not the eggs Mrs. Napier brought here, or I won't eat them." Taking the A&P egg carton and placing it on the counter, my mother went on to prepare homemade biscuits and delicious fried eggs for breakfast. After I completely had finished eating, Mom asked, "How were the eggs this morning? Did you like them?" "Yes, the eggs tasted great just like the eggs from A&P always do. Thank you, Mom." A sheepish grin appeared on my mother's face, and I asked why she was smiling. Remaining mum, Mom went about the business of cleaning the kitchen but her impish grin did not disappear. My suspicion became aroused, and I pried, "Did you fix me those eggs you got from Mrs. Napier?" "Yes, I did," Mom replied, going on to tell me that now I knew that the eggs I ate were the same as those purchased at the A&P and just as tasty.

One family in our neighborhood would often have domestic disagreements that would spill into the community, especially on warm days when their windows and door were opened. The man who lived there with his wife and three children worked in the coal mines on weekdays but liked to visit his relatives who lived several miles away on the weekends. On some weekends, he would be picked up by his brother early Friday evening, after getting home from work and cleaning up, and would not return until late Sunday afternoon. This schedule did not sit well with his wife, who regularly complained to the neighbors that she didn't understand why her husband didn't want to spend his weekends with the immediate family instead of going to his brother's house and "...laying drunk all weekend...." On more than one occasion when the man had not returned home by dark on Sunday, the wife would come to our house and hire my sister, Debbie, to come to her home to watch the kids while she drove the car to look for him. My sister felt sorry for the children, so she reluctantly agreed. Debbie had learned from experience that when the husband and wife returned home, they would already be fighting in the car or would begin fighting upon exiting the vehicle. Mom and Dad had advised my sister that she was to leave the neighbor's house and return home as soon as their car entered the driveway. Upon returning home, Debbie remained frightened for what might happen. Mom always shook her head in dismay, noting that she wished the neighbors could get beyond their disagreements for the sake of the kids. Dad once interjected that the man "...probably wanted to stay drunk to not have to hear his wife nag and berate him all weekend...." Mom was not amused by my father's comment.

Another neighbor, Mr. Wake, had an affinity for the bottle and often could be seen drinking alcoholic beverages while sitting on his front porch. He sometimes would sing aloud while drinking, which my siblings and I found amusing. Mr. Wake had cleaned out the basement at his house and installed a colorful merry-go-round which seated six children and was activated by the riders moving pedals up and down; at least three riders pedaling had to be on board for the fun ride to go round and round. The faster the pedal motion, the faster the ride would turn, creating a carnival-like experience for a kid. Mr. Wake would charge each child who boarded the ride one dime. Benny and I, along with the Howard boys, were frequent customers despite Mom's reluctance to provide us with the money needed for admittance. My mother, a strict tee-totaler, suspected that Mr. Wake might be using the proceeds he collected from the children to support his drinking habit.

One late Saturday afternoon as I returned from walking to Smith's Grocery, I noticed a large object in the ditch across the street from our house. As I walked closer, it became clear that the object was a man who was lying in the ditch and not moving. Hesitant to approach the man, I struggled with what I should do. I decided to move closer and while doing so Mr. Wake's face came into my view. He had his eyes closed and continued to not move. I panicked as I remembered Mrs. Spicer lying totally still in her casket with her eyes shut at the Methodist Church. "Mr. Wake is dead!" I thought. I called to Mr. Wake, and he did not answer which gave credence to my fear. After calling Mr. Wake's name a second time with no answer, I ran as fast as I could inside our house. "Mom, Mom, where are you?" I shouted as I bounded into the kitchen. My mother got up from a chair in the living room asking, "What's wrong? Why are you running and shouting?" "Come quickly!" I exclaimed. "Mr. Wake is lying in the ditch across the street from our house and I think he is dead!" Mom hurriedly walked to her bedroom and peered out the window. Mr. Wake still was lying in the ditch and not moving, just as he was before I came into the house. "Mom, you have got to go outside the house and see. We've got to do something now!" I begged. Mom went back into the living room to tell her sister visiting from Richmond what she had seen. The sisters decided it best if they went outside to investigate the situation further with me remaining in the house. I stationed myself at Mom's bedroom window while she and her sisters made their way outside. I observed what appeared to be them trying to talk to Mr. Wake and wondered why they were talking to a dead person. After a few minutes, Mom and her sister engaged in what appeared to be nothing more than idle chit chat, smiling while they were doing so. I became more agitated that the adults in charge were not taking the situation seriously and remembered what Mom had told me about being respectful around the dead before I accompanied her to Mrs. Spicer's funeral. After several more minutes, the sisters came back into the house continuing their laughter and banter. Outraged, I screamed, "What are you all doing? I can't believe you're laughing at a dead man. I liked Mr. Wake and he was always nice to me." Taken aback by my outburst, Mom replied, "I'm so sorry. We should have come back in sooner to tell you. Mr. Wake isn't dead. He is drunk and had passed out when you saw him earlier." "But he's still in the ditch and not moving!" I argued. My mother assured me that he had moved a few times while they were talking to him and even mumbled a few words. Perhaps not wanting to cause further embarrassment to Mrs. Wake, Mom asked me to let her know that her husband was lying in the ditch by our house. Walking to their house, I felt a sense of relief that the man had not died but was sad that he was so drunk and lying in the dirty ditch. Mrs. Wake openly wept when I told her about Mr. Wake and said that she was at her wits' end with her husband. I didn't know what else to do other than trying to smile while she continued crying and talking to me. An hour or so later, a couple of men who lived near the Wake's came in a car to help Mr. Wake out of the ditch and back to his house.

Dad seldom drove us to church on Sundays or Wednesday evenings. Mom, my siblings, and I would walk, leaving our house early enough to arrive at the church before the bell sounded announcing that the service was about to begin. It was a sunny day this particular Sunday, on the way home from church, and everyone walked quickly thinking about the mouth-watering meal that my Mom would prepare. As we approached John Golden's store, Dawson Market, I noticed that several boys were gathered near the narrow highway that we would take up the hill to reach our house. I soon heard a woman shouting and cursing and watched as some boys yelled, "Go Bonnie! Go Bonnie!" I was walking well ahead of Mom, Debbie, and Bennie with my older brothers, and had a good view of what was taking place. Ronnie told me that he thought the woman was Crazy Bonnie when I saw her pull up her dress to her hips and shout, "Go to hell, boys! You can kiss my ass!" Rather than getting angry at the woman, the boys continued their laughing, taunting her with jeers of, "Go Bonnie! Go Bonnie!" At this point, I became frightened and decided that I would wait up to walk with my mother. When Mom caught up with me, I told her what I had seen and heard. Mom confirmed that the woman's name was Bonnie but was angry that the boys were provoking and irritating her. Mom explained that Bonnie was not well and that the boys should know better than to upset her. I asked my mother if Bonnie had cancer like the little neighbor girl who died. Mom told me that the woman was ill in her mind and had been sent to Radford several times for treatment. Debbie later told me that there was a hospital in Radford that helped people who were sick like Bonnie. I continued to quiz my mother about what she was telling me asking, "Why did Ronnie tell me the woman was Crazy Bonnie?" Sternly Mom told me that Ronnie would be in trouble with her for calling Bonnie crazy and that people who are ill mentally should not be called disrespectful names.

A few months later, when Mom's flowers were in full bloom, I was playing outside while my mother was busy watering them. I saw a woman standing by Mom with her back to me holding several old newspapers and made my way over to see who was visiting. I was petrified when it became clear to me that the woman holding the old newspapers filled with stems of flowers was Bonnie, the angry woman I had seen on the way home from church. I started to run away, and Mom intervened, clutching my hand. "Thomas Lee, can you say hello to Miss Bonnie?" she requested. I said "Hello," still trying very hard to break free of my mother's tight grasp. Mom went on to tell me that Miss Bonnie liked beautiful flowers and that she was sharing some of hers with the woman. As I glanced up to acknowledge Miss Bonnie's presence, the woman smiled at me and commented on how beautiful all my mother's flowers were in full bloom. My fear dissipated somewhat and shortly thereafter Mom released my hand, and I was off to play.

Billy, a young adult man, who lived in Dawson with his mother, could often be seen walking on the streets and highways in the community. Billy had only gone to school a short time before he was withdrawn. Johnny and Ronnie told me that Billy was retarded; Mom, however, said that he was simply slow in doing things and that he was a good-natured man.

Everyone in Dawson knew Billy and liked him. Billy garnered affection by his delightful disposition and ever-present smile. It was easy to look beyond the man's missing teeth while talking with him as his broad smile would usually be accompanied by a gentle pat on the back, conveying a warm sense of acceptance and affirmation. The young man's omnipresence had created a large contingent of friends and admirers who always looked forward to a pleasant conversation. Billy loved soda pop and wouldn't mince words when he sensed an opportunity to enjoy the refreshing beverage.

I had accompanied my father to Dawson Market to pick up a few grocery items for dinner. When the two of us entered the store, we were greeted by the owner, John Golden, who apprised us of whatever special discounts he was offering that particular day. Billy was leaning against the soda pop cooler and wasted no time in greeting the both of us in his usual manner. Dad and I both chatted with him and were ready to continue shopping when he hung his head in a pitiful way and in a disconsolate voice said, "I sure I am thirsty and wish I had a cold Coca-Cola." Dad smiled at Billy and asked why he hadn't already bought himself a soda. Billy responded sadly, "I ain't got no money," maintaining a somber tone. Dad turned to Mr. Golden saying, "Add Billy's Coke to my bill." Billy's despondence immediately turned to joy as he opened the cooler, took out a Coca-Cola, and opened the cap on top of the bottle. After taking a big swig, the young man looked at Dad, thanked him profusely, and told him that he loved him.

Billy's December birthday was known to almost everyone in Dawson. A month or so ahead of the annual event, he would make certain to tell everyone whom he encountered that he would like to have a dollar bill on his birthday. Johnny told me that Billy had bragged about getting over $25 on one of his birthdays. Occasionally, some of the teenage boys in Dawson would tell Billy that his birthday had been taken off the calendar for the year, provoking the young man into a fitful rage of cursing and crying. Mom and Dad always warned my siblings and me about taunting Billy or making light of him in a disrespectful way.

Ronnie told me that Billy's mother had decided to travel to Harveytown one day to pay bills and do some shopping. Before leaving home to wait for the SVTC bus to come, Billy's Mom sternly had told him that he was not to leave the house while she was gone and that he would be in trouble if he chose to do so. No sooner had she exited the bus in Harveytown than she passed Billy standing on the street drinking a C and talking with someone whom he knew. He had hitch-hiked to town and had arrived twenty minutes or so before his mother. Billy's mother was so astonished at her son's ingenuity that she forgot about his disobedience and any punishment that might have been associated with it.

The lives and antics of our neighbors constantly were of interest to me. At some level, I considered them to be part of my family as I was excited to learn of their good fortune and saddened when told of their adversities. My world outside of my immediate family was both expanded and amplified by the bond and connection that I felt for others with whom I shared the community.

6/Dawson School

Talk of closing Creekside School became more frequent and pronounced during 1963. As head teacher at the school, Dad sometimes would be asked to attend meetings in Harveytown with other quasi-administrators and elementary school principals where he would be privy to gossip and speculation related to possible school consolidation. I had overheard my parents discussing how the closing of Creekside School might affect Dad's school assignment and the educational situation for Benny and me. Debbie, Johnny and Ronnie were already attending Camden High School and the closing of Creekside School would have no bearing on their education. After many conversations and thoughtful deliberation, the decision was made that Benny and I would begin attending Dawson School in the fall of the school year.

Dawson School, which was located a block or so from our house, would be close enough for my brother and me to walk to and from. I had walked past the school many times enroute to Smith's Grocery but had only been inside the building when my family received the polio vaccine. The red brick structure was so large that it required four entrances. The school campus appeared massive and housed several swings, a giant slide, and multiple see-saws. A regulation-size basketball area with an asphalt court and goals with nets was situated in front of the school's main entrance. A tether ball pole was adjacent to the school's south entrance and a vast field that included an area for playing baseball was part of the acreage. Teachers' and other staff members' cars were parked in a designated lot beside two school buses. The school stood in stark contrast to Creekside School, which could easily have fit in a single area of the large building.

Benny and I walked by ourselves to school on our first day. We entered the building through the east entrance. I was beginning fourth grade and was taken to Mrs. Golden's classroom by a lady whom I had not seen before. Benny was escorted to Mrs. Lee's classroom that had her name and 3rd grade printed on a sign attached to the doorway. As I walked down the cavernous hallway that seemed to go on forever, the clickety-clack of other kids' shoes on the wide, hardwood floors reverberated in my ears. I entered my classroom after being greeted by Mrs. Golden and took my assigned seat, which had my name printed on a strip of primary writing paper that had been affixed to the desk. I looked about the room to see if I could spot any other kids whom I knew. Luckily, I saw Robert Howard and waved my hand to say hello. He waved back whispering, trying not to draw Mrs. Golden's attention, "I'm glad you are going to be in my room." Beginning to miss my classmates at Creekside School, I silently reflected, "At least there will be one person in my classroom whom I know."

After reading a story to us and making everyone aware of the classroom rules, Mrs. Golden announced that we would be going on a tour of the school. Everyone was asked to line up by the door and wait for the teacher to take her place at the head of the line. Our first stop was the library, a large room located directly across the hallway from the classroom. Mrs. Golden explained to the class that the library was a place where lots of interesting books other than our schoolbooks were amassed, along with magazines, film strips, and movie films. Three walls of the room had large, tall shelves that spanned their width; the shelves were overflowing with books. I never had seen so many books in one place and became so excited I had to remind myself to refrain from taking one from the shelf to examine right then. Colorful book jackets were displayed on the bulletin boards behind a large teacher's desk and a tall counter. Mrs. Golden told everyone that our class would be coming to the library once every two weeks to visit with the librarian, Mrs. Anderson, and to check out two books on loan that we could take home to read! As our class left the library, I began daydreaming about how much fun I would have curled up on the living room couch reading my books and looking at all the pictures.

We continued our tour in the hallway, stopping in front of Mr. Bennett's office. "Mr. Bennett is the principal and person in charge at our school," Mrs. Golden noted. "I guess Mr. Bennett doesn't have to teach and be in charge of the school like Dad does at Creekside," I thought. I figured that the Dawson School was so big that Mr. Golden had to spend all his day just looking after everything. Our class walked past the big set of doors where Benny and I had entered the building earlier in the day and then on down the hallway to another set of doors with big windows. The teacher directed everyone to take a peek through the windows to see the large field where we could run and play during recess and lunch breaks.

We returned to our classroom but did not stop to go inside. Continuing down the hallway, we reached a set of large steps that appeared to lead to the downstairs area of the building. Mrs. Golden led us down two sets of steps and I thought we would never reach the bottom floor. At the bottom of the stairwell, yet another set of double doors led outside. Instead of exiting the building, we turned right and walked straight ahead, entering a very large room that resembled my church. The teacher identified the room as the school's auditorium and told everyone that we would be coming here to watch plays. The only plays I had ever seen were those at my church on Christmas Eve and they always were fun to watch. Different from what was in my church was a large, elevated platform that Mrs. Golden told us was called a stage. The stage had gigantic curtains on each of its sides and I wondered if they opened and closed like the ones at my church that were temporarily put up for the annual Christmas play.

After leaving the auditorium, we all made our way back up all the stairs, stopping at the top to catch our breath. Our teacher then led the class back down the hallway toward the principal's office; stopping short of the office, everyone turned right and walked down two more large sets of steps. Beginning to feel a little tired from all the walking and climbing, I wondered to myself, "How many sets of steps are in this place?" The steps led to another large room that had a pleasing, intoxicating odor. I wondered if someone was baking some of my Mom's yeast rolls that I savored at Sunday dinners. Mrs. Golden told us that we were in the cafeteria and showed the class how we would line up to first go into the kitchen to get our plate of food before taking a seat on one of the long benches connected to all the tables. The longer we stayed in the cafeteria, the hungrier I became smelling the tantalizing aroma of the bread baking in the ovens. On our way out of the cafeteria, I noticed a large television placed on top of an unusually tall metal stand. Thinking that I may get to watch television here, I started liking Dawson School better all the time.

Shortly after everyone returned to the classroom, a bell sounded that was much different than the one I had heard at Creekside School. Mrs. Golden informed us that it was time for recess and that we could leave the classroom without running and make our way outside to the playground. I waited by the door for Robert and asked if I could accompany him outside. "Sure!" he said, "Let's go down the big slide." Recess at Dawson School was no different from what occurred at Creekside School. Kids were running and playing in every place and direction. Robert and l made our way to the slide and waited for our turn in a sizeable line that had formed. Once my turn to go down the slide arrived, I quickly pushed off and sailed to the bottom, again thinking that I was going to like Dawson School, even though I was missing my friends and Dad.

After we returned to the classroom, Mrs. Golden distributed several textbooks that she said we would use each day. I received books for reading, arithmetic, science, social studies and music. The reading book was of the same series I had read at Creekside School and had Ginn and Company printed on its front cover. My arithmetic book had a hard cover and was different from the workbook I could write in at the other school. I didn't know what social studies or science was and would have to wait for Mrs. Golden to tell me what to do with them. The paperback music book was of great interest to me in that it was a novelty as well. I couldn't resist taking a peek inside when the teacher wasn't looking. The music book had lines and notes that Miss. Carnes had taught me about and included words, some of which I could read, like the song books at my church. The cover and pages of the book were very worn and it was difficult to read some of the words. My teacher said the book was very old and made in 1920; I suddenly realized that the book I had in my hands was older than my mother, who was born in 1923. I became even more enlivened during the rest of the morning as Mrs. Golden told the class about lots of other fun things we would do in fourth grade. When the bell sounded for the third time, the teacher announced that it was time for lunch. Lunch period would last for one hour with those eating in the cafeteria lining up at the door and those who had brought a lunch from home or would be walking home for lunch falling in behind them. Robert was in the line for the cafeteria and exited the room earlier than I. Mom had told both Benny and me to wait for each other outside the door we entered in order to walk home together for lunch.

Benny and I met outside the school and hurried home. We talked about our teachers and how different our new school was from the old one; there were so many more books and rooms at Dawson School. However, we both lamented that we missed our friends at Creekside School and wished our Dad was at Dawson School. I told Benny that I would have preferred to eat those delicious-smelling rolls in the cafeteria rather than whatever our Mom might have prepared us to eat at home.

When we arrived home, Mom was waiting for us in the yard smiling. "How did it go this morning? Do you boys like Dawson School?" she inquired. We both told Mom that everything went OK and that we thought we would like the school. Since we were both famished and our appetites were piqued from smelling the rolls baking, we didn't want to linger for more conversation. We promptly went inside the house and sat at the kitchen table. Mom had prepared each of us a tasty grilled cheese sandwich that still smelled of the creamy butter that was used to sear the bread, which had Kraft Velveeta cheese oozing out the middle. I quickly gulped the sandwich down and made my way to the privy for a much-needed visit. When both of us had finished eating and going to the bathroom, we asked if we could return to school to play before the bell rang. Mom hugged us goodbye, and we soon were back at school exploring the swings and slide.

The rest of my first day at Dawson School was spent listening to more stories and trying to learn the names of my classmates. A second recess period came an hour and a half or so after we returned from lunch. When the final bell of the day sounded, announcing the end of the school day, I was ready to get home and take a nap. Robert walked home with Benny and me and we talked about how much fun we would have later in the fall riding the cardboard sleds down the steep hill located behind the

Howards' house. Benny and I excitedly recounted the day's events to everyone at the dinner table and were off to bed early. I mentally charted the fun things I had done at school as I dozed off to sleep for the night.

My year spent in Mrs. Golden's classroom continued to be filled with new and exciting experiences. After we all repeated the Pledge of Allegiance to the American flag each morning, my teacher would collect two cents from everyone who wished to purchase a one-half pint size carton of milk, just as my teachers at Creekside School had done. After giving our teacher the two pennies, my classmates and I would be permitted to color a square by our name on a large chart board affixed to the wall on the side of the classroom. I felt really bad for the kids that did not pay my teacher the two cents because they would have no milk to drink. For a time, I would ponder, "Do their Moms and Dads not have the money to give them for the milk?" or "Maybe they don't like to drink the white milk," that doesn't always taste very good without eating something before taking a drink. One day the small milk cartons that were delivered to our room looked different; the cartons were brown instead of white. Mrs. Golden told everyone that we were about to enjoy a special surprise. When I opened the carton and took a drink of my milk, I immediately was aware that it tasted sweet like chocolate and was very flavorful. I drank the rest of the cold, chocolate-flavored treat pretending that I was eating chocolate ice cream. I felt even sadder now for those classmates that didn't have the pennies to pay for the milk.

Our class was divided into groups for our reading time with Mrs. Golden. After she introduced new words by holding up flashcards, each kid would read a portion aloud from our reading books to the others in the group. Mrs. Golden often told me that I read very well and at times I would need to bite my lip from blurting a word out that had stumped a classmate. Some of my classmates would struggle to pronounce almost all the words in the passage they had been assigned to read. After we dispersed from our group, we returned to our desks to answer questions about the story we had read in our own book in a new workbook that had a cover identical to the one on my reading book. I was glad that we could record our answers in the workbook instead of having to write them on notebook paper. Five or six other kids and I always seemed to finish the workbook assignment before everyone else and would be asked by Mrs. Golden to go to one of the small tables in the back of the room to review the story words on the flashcards with the handful of classmates who struggled to read. I thought it was a lot of fun to pretend to be the teacher, like my Dad or Mrs. Golden.

Being on the playground during recess was a favorite part of my day. In addition to being able to enjoy the swings, slide, and see-saws, there were many more kids to play "hide-and-go-seek," "cowboys and Indians," or "cops and robbers". Having such a large playground made the high-adventure games more suspenseful and realistic. As I was running furiously around the school one day, chasing another boy in a game of "cops and robbers", I rounded a corner of the building and squarely butted heads with a kid running in the opposite direction. I felt a giant thump and the next thing I remembered was lying on the ground with four or five other kids staring down at me. One cried out, "I think we need to go get Mr. Bennett. He's hurt bad!" I opened my eyes, now feeling a fierce pounding in my head, and reached out my arm to someone asking them to help me stand. I was able to walk back to the classroom where Mrs. Golden checked me over and had someone go to the cafeteria to get ice for me to hold on a big bump that had appeared near the top of my head. The ice seemed to help the headache after a time, and I was beginning to look forward to eating my lunch.

During our arithmetic class time before lunch period, we recited our multiplication tables and labored over long division problems that would require dividing a six-digit number by a four-digit number. I tried to conserve my school supplies, just as my parents had asked me to do, but the algorithms made it necessary for me to use one whole side of a piece of notebook paper to complete one division problem. Again, if I finished early (which was seldom when assigned to complete long division problems), I was asked to assist my classmates in learning their multiplication tables.

After everyone returned from lunch, Mrs. Golden would allow us to rest our heads on the desktop while she read an engaging story with such ardor and diction that my mind could travel to the setting with little effort. My attention was especially riveted by her reading of *Charlotte's Web* and my disappointment was mixed with anticipation when she said, "That's all for today. We'll have to wait until tomorrow to see what will happen next."

Having access to the school library opened up a world outside of Dawson for me. I read every version of *The Boxcar Children* and *Henry Huggins* in the library's collection. Biographies of *Babe Ruth* and *George Washington Carver* became repetitive reads for me.

Our science and social studies lessons allowed everyone in the class to talk and ask lots of questions. Mrs. Golden told us that social studies was about people and places, some people whom we might know and others whom we did not and who lived far away. It was fun for me to have a turn examining the large conch shell that was part of her collection of science materials. Mrs. Golden explained that if one held the large shell to an ear, they might hear sounds of the ocean. I had read about and seen pictures of an ocean in my books but had never visited one. The sea looked like an exciting place to be from the pictures I had seen of kids like me walking on sandy beaches looking for shells to put in colorful pails.

Mrs. Golden would sometimes get upset when one of my classmates or I would not follow her directions. While everyone was working on arithmetic problems, our instructions were not to talk with each other. A boy sitting across from me kept talking about how much fun it would be for two or three kids to go down the big playground slide together. Mrs. Golden already had verbally admonished the two of us twice. When we began to talk a third time, my classmate and I were asked to come to the teacher's desk, being advised that we were about to receive a third reminder that we were supposed to be working on our arithmetic problems without talking. Bending my hand by clasping all my fingers in the palm of her hand, Mrs. Golden swatted the palm of my hand three times with her paddle, and I felt a sting that I did not soon forget. Blinking back tears, I returned to my seat thinking, "I hate Mrs. Golden! I thought she was a nice teacher." Several minutes later, my teacher appeared at my desk and whispered in my ear, "Thomas Lee, I don't like to spank boys and girls. You must learn to obey the classroom rules." Still feeling betrayed, I remained mad at my teacher until the end of the school day when I admitted to myself, "Mrs. Golden had warned me to stop talking twice before I got the spanking. I should have listened better and obeyed the rules, and I would not have gotten in trouble."

Music time in the classroom was a fun part of the day which I eagerly anticipated. Everyone would sing songs in unison from our book with Mrs. Golden leading us from the front of the room. With our mouths open widely we would sing:

Susie, little Susie, now what is the news?
The geese are going barefoot because they've no shoes.
The cobbler has leather, but no lace has he,
And he cannot make them new shoes don't you see.

All my classmates and I always enjoyed bellowing out songs that could be sung as a round. Everyone would get to move their arms back and forth at our seats while singing:

Row, row, row your boat
Gently down the stream,
Merrily, merrily, merrily, merrily,
Life is but a dream.

Another favorite tune that I often sang in my head long after the music period had ended was "Uncle Ned." One of the kids in my classroom had asked Mrs. Golden why Uncle Ned was called a darkie; she explained that colored people sometimes were called darkies. I did not fully understand about Uncle Ned and why he had a shovel and hoe and frequently would wonder where he had gone.

There was an old darkie and his name was
Uncle Ned and he died long ago, long ago,

*He had no wool on the top of his
head in the place where the wool ought to grow.
So, lay down the shovel and hoe, pick up the fiddle and the bow.
For there's no more work for poor old Ned,
he's gone where the good darkies go.*

One day as we gathered our school supplies and library books right before the bell would ring announcing the end of the school day, a thunderous buzzing noise sounded throughout the school building. The noise was interrupted intermittently, with a brief pause between each burst of sound, and we recognized the sound to be the fire alarm. Mrs. Golden seemed alarmed asking everyone to form a line quickly to exit the building. Our teacher had provided us with instructions previously on the route we were to take to go outside. After everyone was in the hallway, Mr. Bennett told Mrs. Golden that she would not be accompanying her class out their assigned exit but would leave the building from another door. The classmate at the front of the line led everyone down the hallway and then down the two flights of steps, our customary fire drill exit path. At the bottom of the steps, I saw a large chain that had been placed on the two big doors that we were to open in order to go outside. The school's custodian was stationed by the doors along with another man whom I did not recognize. "How are we supposed to go outside?" one kid asked. Both men shrugged their shoulders to indicate, "I don't know," without speaking a word. After waiting for a few minutes, a couple of boys tried to push the doors open ignoring the chains; the doors would not budge. One of the girls pleaded, "We need to go outside, or we all will be in trouble. Mrs. Golden told us that we couldn't always know if we were having a drill or if the school was actually on fire." "I want to go outside!" another girl exclaimed. The two adults continued to stand at the door remaining mum. Trying to figure out our conundrum, I reflected on how my teacher had inculcated me, and everyone else, to respect the school's rules or risk getting into big trouble, yet we were physically unable to follow our normal fire drill rule. Hoping that my disobedience would be overlooked, I suggested that my beleaguered classmates and I should go and see if we could get out of the building using the door by the stage in the auditorium. Everyone treaded gingerly toward the exit by the stage, hoping that we would not be in trouble with our teacher for going out the wrong door. The door opened and everyone made their way outside where Mrs. Golden and Mr. Bennett were waiting. All at once, several classmates of mine began telling the two of them about the doors being chained and how we only took the wrong door because we couldn't exit using the assigned one. Our principal and teacher both smiled and told everyone that they did the right thing and that they were very proud of us.

I enjoyed listening to Mr. Bennett's deep, resounding voice coming from the intercom located above the chalkboard at the front of the room; he always would begin any announcement by saying, "Would you pardon me, please?" before providing communication to the entire school. When the principal's voice came into my classroom on November 22, 1963, something sounded different before he went on to say, "I am sorry to have to tell everyone that our President, John F. Kennedy, was shot in Dallas, Texas, this afternoon. I don't have any more information at this time but will let everyone know if there is more news regarding this." "Oh no! I hope he didn't get killed!" one of the girls in the back of the room said aloud. Another girl seated across from me began to cry. I looked at the front of the room to get assurance from Mrs. Golden, but she was standing frozen with both hands covering her mouth. Regaining her composure, Mrs. Golden told everyone that we could put our social studies books away and that she would read us a story; as she began to read, my mind could not be distracted from what I had heard. Questions raced through my head, and I was not sure that everyone and everything was OK; I wanted to be home with Mom and Dad. Mr. Bennett later came back on the intercom to inform everyone that President Kennedy had died and that it was a sad day for our country. I was glad that the school day almost was over when word came that our president was dead, so everyone could go home to be with their families.

Sometimes, my mother would need to be away from the house during my lunch period or would not have anything readily available that she could prepare for Benny and me, so we ate lunch in the cafeteria. On these occasions, I continued to wonder about the big television on the tall rolling stand. One morning, Mrs. Golden had told everyone that a special treat awaited us and that we needed to work to finish our reading groups before the principal made a special announcement. When Mr. Bennett finally did speak through the intercom this time, every ear in the classroom was attentively attuned to the words he uttered. A sea of smiles could be seen across my classroom when it was announced that everyone would be assembling in the cafeteria to watch a gigantic rocket lift off into space.

After the teacher assembled everyone in the hallway, we made our way down the steps to the cafeteria. The older kids, who were in the upper grades, were already in the room and seated at the tables where we ate lunch. Mrs. Golden directed us to our seats and told us to be quiet until everyone had assembled in the room. The kids from the lower grades filed into the room, with those who were in first grade having to sit on the floor in the front of the room since all available seats had been taken. Mr. Bennett went to the big television set and turned the round knob to the ON position; when the black-and-white picture appeared on the screen, he increased the volume significantly allowing everyone to hear what was taking place. Within minutes, everyone could see the large capsule that would be NASA's largest launch vehicle ever to enter outer space. Astonished faces of adults and kids alike reflected what they were witnessing on the television as the fiery rocket engines roared, propelling a vehicle into the air that eventually would orbit the Earth in space. The television coverage continued for several more minutes as I, along with everyone else in the room, followed the camera's depiction of the space vehicle so high in the sky that it could hardly be seen. What seemed like way too soon, we all returned to our classrooms, still excited and wanting to discuss and ask lots of questions about what we had seen.

The spring of the year ushered in the Easter season and thoughts of summer vacation. Mrs. Golden planned a large egg hunt in her yard that was located near Dawson School. Everyone in my classroom was asked to bring three boiled eggs from home; the eggs were colored on the big table in the back of the room with each kid getting a turn to choose the color of dye in which he or she would dip an egg. Mrs. Golden designated one egg as special, calling it the lucky egg, and announced that the kid who found the lucky egg would win a prize of five dollars. After all the eggs had been dyed and were dry, they were placed in large woven baskets that our teacher had brought from her home. Some of the older boys and girls, who were in the 8th grade, came to our classroom to take the eggs to the Goldens' big yard for hiding. When instructed to do so, everyone lined up and made their way out of the building to travel to the Golden's yard. I was wishing hard that I would be the kid to find the lucky egg. Although I managed to find several eggs, another kid found the lucky one and garnered the coveted prize.

As the days grew warmer and I could feel the soft breezes through the open windows in the classroom, it became increasingly difficult to focus on things like arithmetic, science and even reading. Mrs. Golden seemed to be in a hurry to have us finish our reading and arithmetic books and grew frustrated when we had difficulty paying attention for long periods of time. The school year soon ended, and summer vacation arrived, allowing me to spend most of my days playing outdoors.

7/Growing Up

I began my fifth grade of school feeling totally ungrounded as a consequence of a crushing event that had occurred during summer vacation. Even though I was glad to see school resume so I could be with my friends, a sense of emptiness was my constant companion. My new classroom was a single-wide, mobile unit that had been located on the campus to accommodate the school's growth. Mrs. Small, a relatively young woman, whose husband taught at another school in the county, was my assigned teacher. She enjoyed teaching activities that involved the kids moving about the classroom, which wasn't an easy feat in such a narrow space. Spelling bees had everyone standing along the side walls of the room and being given a word to correctly spell aloud; if the word was spelled correctly, one was allowed to continue the game, whereas if a word was misspelled, he or she had to return to their desk. I always was competitive while participating in the spelling bees but managed to be the only kid who remained standing a couple of times during the school year.

Social studies projects were assigned to my classmates and me, requiring that we complete research on one of the fifty states of the union and write a report. Additionally, the project required a presentation to the class using creative visual aids. Having been assigned Alaska, I was envious of a classmate who had been assigned Hawaii; I had wanted to be assigned Hawaii, so I could make a pretend volcano, like one I had seen my Dad make at home, to be my creative aid. Mrs. Small appeased my disappointment by suggesting that I create an igloo and bring some of Dad's Indian paraphernalia to school as part of my presentation. I finally did become somewhat excited about my assignment when Mrs. Small told me that she would purchase a couple of boxes of sugar cubes during her Saturday grocery shopping trip for me to use to construct the igloo and that I could eat what I didn't use on the project.

The Beatles became wildly popular in the mid-1960s after appearing on *The Ed Sullivan Show*, which was broadcast on Sunday nights. My brother Johnny had small, 45 RPM phonograph records of some of the Beatles' hit songs which I had heard repeatedly played on the family's record player located in our basement. The school was hosting a variety show that would take place in the auditorium and each classroom had been requested to provide an act. Mrs. Small, always full of creativity, asked me and three other boys in the class if we would dress as the Beatles and pantomime singing one of their hit tunes as our contribution to the show. We all agreed and began searching for costumes at home and in the neighborhood; four dark-colored wigs were located that we would wear to mimic the Beatles' long hair when we pretended to be singing while a recording of the song was played on the school's record player. I was assigned the role of Ringo Starr and brought one of my Dad's old drums that he used as part of his scouting projects. The act was well-received by everyone at the school; many kids in the audience stood and screamed until the curtain closed – just like *The Ed Sullivan Show*.

A large propane storage tank was located in the large playground field near one of the old buildings that was being used as an overflow classroom. The tank had curved metal handles on its top that were located at each end of the reservoir, making it easy for kids to play on the structure by grasping with their hands and pulling their bodies up to its top. I liked to pretend that the storage tank was a giant spaceship on which I could use to move through space. I had begun to notice that if I was having difficulty pulling my body to the top of the tank, but continued trying to pull up, that I would get an unusual, extremely pleasurable sensation after several minutes. This pleasurable experience, that had happened a couple of times, so aroused my curiosity that I asked Mrs. Small about it one day after recess had ended. She answered by looking at me with a puzzled look and stern face saying, "Thomas Lee, you don't need to be concerned about that for now." Later that evening, I told Ronnie about my discovery and asked him if he could tell me why it happened. Ronnie just shook his head disgustedly and said, "You better stop doing that or you'll get in big trouble." Another occurrence of something happening to me that I did not understand, and no one would explain to me, only added to my frustration.

News came to our school that a colored boy would begin attending in a week or so. I was excited and hoped that the kid would be fun like the ones with whom I had ridden the bus home from Creekside School. My older siblings had heard at the high school that a television station from Bristol, Tennessee, would be coming to the school on the day the new student was to arrive. It was morning recess time when the boy arrived at the school with his grandfather. The grandfather was a distinguished-looking gentleman dressed in a suit and tie and the kid got out of the car with a big smile on his face. The bell to return to class rang and I did not hear any more about the situation until Benny and I were walking home from school. Benny told me that the boy was in his classroom and that he had talked to him and liked him. I couldn't understand why a television station would be at our school simply because a new student had enrolled.

I became friends with Robby in fifth grade and learned that he lived nearby, just a few blocks away from me. Robby's favorite pastime was sports and he, too, listened to the Virginia State basketball games on the radio. Robby, good natured albeit quite reserved, was an intelligent boy and the two of us often would talk about things we were learning in school. Walking home for lunch one day, he asked what I thought I would have to eat, and I told him that I hoped it would be a grilled cheese sandwich. He began to weep and told me that he would be having pinto beans again, having already been served them for several meals running because that was the only food his family had. Robby's Dad had served in battle, receiving a serious head wound during the war. I told my Mom what Robby had said to me and when I returned home from school that afternoon, she gathered several food items for me to take to Robby's home. Mom later told me that Robby's mother had come to our house to thank her for the food and to tell her that it came at just the right time.

My first experience with having a male teacher was in the sixth grade. Mr. Napier was a tall man who always appeared dapper with his starched-and-pressed white dress shirts, just like those worn by my Dad, and a stylish crew cut that outlined his receding hairline. I had been warned by my classmates and my older siblings that he was a hard teacher and not someone whom anyone would want to make cross. Mr. Napier lived on a small farm and would have the school cafeteria staff put the lunch leftovers in large metal buckets for him to take home each day to feed his hogs. A half hour or so before the end of the school day, two boys in my class would leave the room to go to the cafeteria and carry the slop buckets to his well-used truck that was parked in the teachers' lot. My teacher had told us that his pigs really liked the left-over milk the slop buckets contained and would grow fatter and fatter as they ate it.

I had a terrible fear of Mr. Napier's paddle, which he kept displayed on the top of his desk for all to see. The paddle was made from a board of hard wood and showed evidence of having some age. I was the recipient of the much-feared board only one time over the course of the school year when a classmate and I were spotted by Mr. Napier running in the hallway to make it back inside after remaining outside too long after the bell had rung to end afternoon recess. Several of the kids in my class were not as lucky as I. I witnessed many of the same classmates being spanked several times for their recalcitrance with respect to obeying classroom rules. Still dealing with the dejection that had besieged me the previous year, I longed to please Mr. Napier and worked very hard to behave and complete my school assignments at a notable level in order to earn good grades. During times when I was scolded or admonished, it seemed that it no longer was possible for me to feel confident and in control of myself.

Mr. Napier's favorite subject to teach was social studies. He had designed a plethora of engaging visual aids that had been used over the years to make our study of different countries throughout the world come alive. While studying the period of the Middle Ages, large, elaborately-detailed colored pencil drawings on poster board were on display throughout the room. A huge three-dimensional model of a medieval castle, complete with decorative flags and surrounded by a large moat, was constructed on one of the tables in the back of the classroom. With both anticipation and anxiety, I looked forward to the comprehensive test that was given at the end of each unit. The unit tests were eight to ten pages and contained a mix of multiple choice, fill-in-the-blank, short answer, and discussion questions along with a map that required one to label important cities, places, rivers, and seas. I would begin preparing for the test at least a week before the Friday on which it was administered. Mr. Napier created fierce competition among the quick-to-learn students by returning the scored tests to everyone beginning with the lowest score and ending with the highest score. Although I usually was in the top five highest scores, having my test returned last only happened once. The test covered material we had studied while learning about Spain and Portugal, and I squirmed in my seat with my heart racing when everyone had received their test back with the exception of me and one other classmate. Mr. Napier tantalized me by appearing to walk toward me when only two tests remained in his hand, but then turned and returned a test to the other kid. Then he returned the one remaining test to me with a smile saying, "Good job!" I quickly opened my test, which had been folded vertically, to discover that I had made a score of 100.

Even though I enjoyed the fierce competition associated with making the highest grade on the social studies unit tests, I never escaped feeling sorry for three of my classmates who consistently had their tests returned first. Although they changed rank order on occasion, everyone in the class knew that these three boys always would be among the first to receive their tests back from Mr. Napier. I could not understand why the boys did not pretend to be sick on the days when tests were returned so their parents would let them stay home from school.

Along with my other classmates, I frequently volunteered to take the chalkboard erasers outside for a dusting especially on days when the classroom was unusually warm. Dusting the erasers meant that I would be excused from my class work for a time, along with getting some comfort from any cool breeze that might be blowing. I would extend the time for as long as I could without raising the suspicion of my teacher. Mr. Napier liked to have the erasers cleaned in late afternoon so as to be ready for any writing that he would do on the chalkboard the next day. Another near-the-end-of-day chore that would need to be completed once a week was the distribution of an oily sawdust compound on the floors of the classroom. Everyone would be asked to store all books and other belongings in their seats before two kids in the room would have the privilege of removing the lid off a large canister in the back of the room and transferring the compound to buckets. Scoops of the compound then would be scattered on the floor of the entire classroom as the helpers made their way up and down the rows of desks. Although I liked being the helper, I didn't look forward to being at my seat while the compound was distributed because the small shavings always made their way into my shoes.

During the long lunch period, Mr. Napier and Mr. Carter, another male teacher at the school, would serve as captains for a game of touch football that was played on the basketball court. I had only seen football played by occasionally watching the NFL on television on Sundays with my Dad at my grandparents' house. I didn't understand much about the game but it looked like fun, with guys in metal helmets dressed in suits with numbers printed on them, chasing and tackling one another. The football played at Dawson School was different in that there were no uniforms, and nobody got tackled. Instead, players would line up against one another and the teacher would throw the football in the air to one of his players who would try to catch it and then run away from the player chasing him; sometimes the player on the opposing team would run in front of his opponent, catching the ball and then running in the opposite direction. If a player running with the ball was tagged by an opponent, play would stop, and the two teams would line up where the player had been tagged to continue the game. On most days, only the boys in seventh grade and eighth grade would participate. A few times, Mr. Napier invited students in his classroom to play the game, telling us that he wanted to give all the boys a chance to participate. I was excited as I lined up and was told by Mr. Napier to run to the center line of the court and look around for a pass; even though I did what I was told, I couldn't hold on to the football. Another player shouted for all to hear, "He can't catch a football. Don't throw it to him, Mr. Napier!" Although I participated in the games a couple more times, I did not enjoy the activity, always being worried that I couldn't catch the ball and would be embarrassed again. I did, however, become motivated to learn the skill that some of my friends had acquired.

My friend, Robby, who was in Mr. Carter's classroom, told me that he had gotten a football for Christmas. He invited me to come to his house after school to pass the ball back and forth. Mom consented for me to go to Robby's house with a warning that I should not stay over one hour. Robby was very skilled at catching and throwing the football, much more so than I. I longed to be able to catch an over-the-shoulder pass like my friend, who would ask me to throw the football well out in front of him while he raced toward the ball pulling it down from the air and securing it next to his chest while he continued running. Robby agreed to try to teach me the skill, but my early attempts were a colossal failure. For several weeks, Robby and I would work on the skill after we had tossed the ball back and forth and I had watched my friend pull multiple over-the-shoulder passes out of the air with complete accuracy.

One afternoon after I had failed at repeated attempts to catch Robby's passes, I was almost ready to concede defeat. Sharing my feeling with my friend, he listened and encouraged me not to quit. Changing the strategy of running a distance of thirty or forty yards to try and pull the football out of the air, Robby asked me to run only ten or fifteen yards while he lobbed the ball more slowly and higher into the air. It happened! I caught the first pass with a shorter run! Robby was excited for me, and I didn't want to stop the fun when my hour of play had ended. I had hoped to try my new skill out by playing in one of lunch period games at school, but Mr. Napier and Mr. Carter only played with the seventh and eighth grade boys for the remainder of the school year. I would enjoy showing off my ability to catch an over-the-shoulder pass in football games when I was allowed to play on the school's field after school.

Both girls and boys participated in other games I enjoyed playing during recess and extended lunch periods. Dodge ball, "Red Rover," and softball were popular favorites among my classmates and me. Tether ball was a game I had never heard of before attending Dawson School. A large ball tethered to a rope was suspended from a metal post and opposing players worked feverishly to be the first to wind the rope completely around the pole. Since only two kids could play at one time, there almost always was a long wait to play the winner of the previous match.

During late spring of each year, the seventh grade and eighth grade boys at the school would play host to another elementary school in the area for a softball game. All students at the school were invited to be spectators at the games by bringing ten cents from home for admission. I always looked forward to the extra outdoors period especially since the classroom could get very warm during that time of day. On days that I had forgotten to ask Mom for ten cents, or a dime wasn't available for me to have, I, along with all other students who were not going outside to the game, assembled in the auditorium with our arithmetic books and were required to compete long division problems. I would be quite angry sitting in the warm classroom with little to no air circulation knowing that my classmates and friends had been allowed to go outside to play or watch the game. Often, I would reflect on why one had to pay a dime for the privilege of getting to participate in something fun instead of being punished by having to do extra schoolwork.

I ate in the cafeteria more often in sixth grade than I previously had. I didn't really know why, since my Mom would be at home on many of the days I didn't have my lunch there. Each Friday of the week, the school cafeteria served the much-anticipated bag lunches. I always pleaded with my mother to let me eat in the cafeteria on Fridays and much of the time I was granted my wish. No one ate their lunch in the cafeteria on bag lunch day as it was reserved for cleaning and sanitizing the space. The pre-prepared bags were arranged on two large tables with one being handed to each kid as he or she made their way through the cafeteria. On warm, pleasant days, I would find a shady place outside to enjoy my lunch; during inclement weather I would return to my classroom desk to eat. While opening the bag, one immediately could smell the delicious aroma of a hot dog wrapped in waxed paper and topped with flavorful meat sauce and an abundance of chopped onions. A colossal hunk of peanut butter fudge, made from USDA-donated peanut butter and white powdered sugar, was in the bottom of the bag, along with an apple and a one-half pint carton of chocolate milk. I always savored every delicious bite of my lunch and on occasion the ladies, who worked in the cafeteria, would give us a second hot dog when there was a surplus.

From time to time, I would linger at the school after the day had ended to play on the playground with some of my friends who lived within walking distance of the building. My friends and I would observe some of the boys in eighth grade playing cards for money behind one of the buildings located in the giant field. If we were seen, the poker players would scare us away by shouting, "Get out of here or we'll kick your ass! And you better not tell on us!" We never lingered after being threatened. On one occasion, one of the boys playing poker called another player a cheater and dared him to a fight; the challenged boy obliged, and a scuffle began. I didn't witness any punches thrown but did see the boys wrestling on the ground. A man walking down the street observed what was taking place and made his way over to the boys. "Stop that fighting now! Every single one of you boys had better get up and get your butts home now. I'm going to stop and tell Mr. Bennett what you boys have been up to. Get out of here now!" The fighting ceased immediately, and the boys quickly gathered their belongings and began running as fast as they could in order not to be identified for a severe punishment from Mr. Bennett and their parents.

My older brothers and some other kids had told me about a boy who attended our school who had earlier been sent away to a reform school located a far distance from Dawson. I had never heard of a reform school and when inquiring about it was told that it was like a jail for kids who had done really bad things. I did not know the boy well enough to talk to him but had seen him on the playground. He had a paper route after school and would stack all the newspapers in a large metal basket located on the front of his bicycle. One day after school, another boy was running on the playground and accidentally knocked the parked bicycle over, causing some of the papers to fall on the ground. Hearing the noise and seeing what had happened, the owner of the bike came over and immediately pushed the boy to the ground and began choking his neck; the boy being choked was both younger and smaller than his assailant and pleaded with him to stop, telling him he couldn't breathe. The choking continued despite his pleas until a teacher came around the corner, breaking the altercation up and telling both boys that they would be talking with Mr. Bennett very soon.

A highlight of attending Dawson School was being part of the excitement and activities occurring both before and during the annual Halloween Carnival. Weeks before the festival each classroom would nominate a king and queen candidate who would coordinate other classmates' efforts to raise funds for the school's Parent-Teacher Association (PTA). My classmates and I were asked to bring something to school to sell to other kids, with the proceeds going toward the fundraising efforts. A variety of treats would be offered for sale during recess and lunch periods, including such delectables as peanut butter roll, home-made fudge, popcorn balls, cookies, and suckers. The class raising the most money would see their nominees crowned as royalty and receiving cash prizes as the last activity of the night at the carnival. The carnival itself offered an array of amusements including a fish pond, grab bag table, cake walk, fortune telling booth, costume contests, and a movie shown in the dark of the school's auditorium. My first foray into romance occurred when I asked a girl in my class to go to the movie with me. We sat next to each other and held hands for a time. The teacher running the projector had difficulty getting the picture and sound synchronized and the volume was so soft that no one could hear what was being said. Any undiscovered romantic feeling soon gave way to boredom and frustration, and we decided to leave the room and return to some of the game booths.

The Halloween carnival was a community affair, drawing young and old alike with its festive atmosphere and spirit of competition. Usual standards of behavior at school, enforced by our teachers and Mr. Bennett, were often ignored in all of the excitement. One carnival night, I watched a Deputy Sheriff had to handcuff and remove a man who was drunk and causing a disturbance. It was not uncommon to hear my classmates talk about a fight that was supposed to take place in the school's parking lot.

8 / Visiting with Grandparents

Absolutely nothing could give me the self-motivation to get out of bed early like knowing that I would be visiting my grandparents for a day or an overnight trip. My siblings and I called my maternal grandmother "Momma Poe," which was only a slight variation on the moniker "Momma" that was used by my mother and her siblings. My maternal grandfather, Ronald, had died from stomach cancer before I was born; having served in World War I, he spent the end of his life in a veterans' hospital. I had heard the story of Mom visiting her father at a veterans' hospital in Virginia shortly before his death. My mother described the medical facility as being "...clean as a pin and having doctors and nurses who were kind to patients and visitors...." Mom always said her last visit with her Dad was bittersweet, in that she knew he was dying, but that the compassionate attention he was receiving at the hospital was exceptional, comforting her that her father was receiving good care. My mother talked often of her childhood and the affection she had for her parents.

Momma Poe was a kind-hearted woman who always wanted to greet me with a hug that I was more than willing to receive. She always wore a dress and kept her hair pinned on the back of her head in a bun. While getting a hug from Momma Poe, my head would only reach to the belt around her waist and I always could smell the wonderful food odors that had permeated the fabric of her garment. My grandmother loved to cook and had logged lots of practice over the years, being charged with meal preparation for her eight children. Momma Poe's kitchen was large enough to house a table and chairs, storage areas, a refrigerator, and a double-basin sink; in one corner of the room was a relatively large, wood-burning cook stove which had always interested me. The black stove was made of cast iron and had four burners on its top; the burners could be lifted or removed by attaching a hand-held metal handle underneath the iron discs. I frequently watched my grandmother lift two of the burners that were not being used for cooking and use a long, metal poker to stoke the fire; this would increase the combustion of the wooden logs and elevate the stove's temperature. The firebox on the stove was positioned below the burners and I was fascinated with how Momma Poe would carry kindling and larger pieces of wood in a coal bucket from outside to keep the fire going. The baking oven was located adjacent to the firebox and my grandmother would always make a fuss about it not being able to maintain a steady temperature, especially when she was baking a cake.

I loved eating at Momma Poe's, where I often would be served cornbread with a pat of butter, fried potatoes, and sometimes a portion of meat; she gave me green beans since I did not like the pinto beans she usually served. The beverage selection never changed: a glass of ice-cold sweet milk that had been delivered to the house earlier in the day by Biltmore Dairy. Mom and Momma Poe referred to the milk I always drank as sweet milk; the milk they preferred, which tasted spoiled to me, was buttermilk. Mom would always eat the pinto beans and accentuated her entrée with a fresh green onion when they were available from the vegetable garden.

My cake serving was usually higher on one side than the other due to what my grandmother described with disappointment as "...too much temperature change in the oven...." However, the cake and boiled icing both were delicious, and I loved the taste of them in my mouth with the cold milk.

My grandmother's bedroom contained a treadle sewing machine that she, just as my mother, would use to mend clothes and construct new garments. The object in the bedroom in which I was most interested was the telephone. Sometimes the telephone would ring during my visits to Momma Poe's, and I would be all ears as my grandmother picked up the receiver and announced, "Poes." I often could infer with whom my grandmother was talking from the conversation I was hearing. When I thought it safe to do so without being caught, I would sneak into the bedroom and listen by lifting the telephone's receiver in hopes of being able to hear other voices, some of whom I might recognize as being my neighbors. One time I was deterred from my eavesdropping when I had the receiver off the hook too long and a voice said, "Number please?" Out of fear, I did not respond to the voice and simply froze in place. After a period of time the voice asked, "Mrs. Poe, are you OK? Do you need something?" Again, I did not respond but managed to replace the receiver on the telephone hook. I left the room thinking I would be in big trouble if the telephone operator told my grandmother of the incident.

I did not visit Momma Poe nearly as often as I did my paternal grandparents. Momma Poe still had two children living at her house and my mother limited our visits, hoping not to add to her mother's workload and strain. My trips to my grandmother's house at Sulpher Creek were exclusively day visits in that there was no extra bedroom space for house guests. My father rarely accompanied us on visits but on occasion would drive Mom, my siblings, and me from our house. Our preferred mode of transportation was to walk the fairly short distance via the railroad tracks that ran parallel to US 24. My siblings and I always relished the opportunity to balance ourselves by walking on one rail of the track, making a game of who could travel the farthest without falling off. Occasionally, I would see blocks of black coal that had fallen from one of the passing trains transporting the commodity to a distant city. Mom and Dad always warned us to be on the lookout for snakes that enjoyed the warmth that the iron tracks and gravel between the wooden cross-ties provided.

Momma Poe's house was located fairly close to a working coal mine. Although I could not see the entrance to the mine from the house, the noise from the machinery operating from the top of the mountain made it difficult for me to hear while I played in the yard. The mine was a forbidden place for my siblings and me to visit due to safety hazards.

Located in front of the house was Sulpher Creek, a stream with a wide bed that contained rocks and stones of varied sizes. The depth of the water in the creek was usually no more than a foot, making it a great place for kids to enjoy walking across its span by stepping on the larger rocks. Frogs, salamanders and minnows called the creek home. The salamanders liked to sunbathe on the larger rocks that were not totally submerged in water. Sometimes I would catch the slimy reptile, only to have it slither out of my hand to make a quick escape. My brothers and I sometimes tried to trap minnows using an empty tin can or paper milk carton with little to no success.

Momma Poe raised a large vegetable garden each year, sometimes having the soil plowed by an acquaintance who used a mule and wooden plow to till the earth. Mom often would work in the garden with my grandmother, hoeing or pulling weeds that might rob the vegetable plants of the water and nutrients contained in the fertile soil. A few times I assisted with picking green beans from the vines that twisted around tall wooden stakes; my contribution to the harvest routinely did not last very long since I did not like the heat and the flying bugs that would buzz in my face. I had learned that if I persisted in complaining, Mom would release me from my job, and I could return to a more pleasurable activity such as playing in the creek.

When my brother Ronnie would come along for the visit, he and my aunt would enjoy playing together. I often attempted to tag along with them since their stories and laughter were quite entertaining. The older kids did not want to be bothered with me and would not hesitate to tell me to "Go away!" or "Go play somewhere else." On one visit while my mother and grandmother traveled into town, my aunt and Ronnie were charged with babysitting me since they were older than I. As soon as the adults had gone, they asked me to take off both of my shoes in order to play a fun game with them. I was reticent to do so but when I saw them remove their own shoes, I complied with their request. No sooner had I removed my shoes than the two of them ran toward me scooping them up; they then returned to put their own shoes back on before running to a distant tree with my shoes. "Come back here! You two have tricked me!" I screamed. I watched as Ronnie tied my shoelaces together and then threw my shoes high into the tree where they rested on a small branch. "Look at what you've done! Now I won't be able to get my shoes down from the tree!" I pleaded. They made no effort to try to retrieve my shoes and ignored my petition, continuing to laugh and joke with each other. Even "I'm telling on you two when Mom and Momma Poe get back home. You'll be in big trouble," elicited no change in my aunt's and Ronnie's demeanor. Shortly before my mother and grandmother returned, I was offered a nickel not to tell on the two tricksters. I took the coin and promised I would not tell if they would bring me my shoes. Ronnie climbed the tree and retrieved my shoes and as soon as I saw that the adults had returned, I ran as quickly as I could to tell them what had happened to me. I didn't return the nickel and later used it to purchase a soda pop at Smith's Grocery.

I referred to my paternal grandparents as "Mamaw" and "Papaw", designations commonly used throughout mainstream Appalachia. I had the distinct and prized honor, at least in their minds, of being their first grandchild, whom they dearly loved, and they spared no expense of their life energy or resources showing it.

My earliest recollection of visiting my Mamaw and Papaw was in a house owned by the coal company where my grandfather worked at Coalgap in Roane County. Although the post office officially designated the community as Coalgap, many of the residents in the neighborhood referred to the place as Big Gap. In the early 1960s, Coalgap was home to a working coal mine which was the primary or ancillary place of employment for the entire community. The company that operated the coal mine had constructed most of the homes, called camp houses, in Coalgap where employees, in times past, were required to live. A large commissary and postal facility was constructed by the mining company and was the hub of social activity for the residents. A bath house that was used by the miners was located adjacent to the commissary building. A Presbyterian church occupied a beautiful brick building with stained-glass windows and a tall steeple where a large metal bell was housed.

My grandparents' house was modest in size and looked almost identical to the other camp houses in Coalgap. The house had a large porch, at least from my perspective, with a swing where my Mamaw and I would sit during the day while Papaw was sleeping; my grandfather worked the evening shift at the coal mine and would not arrive home until after 11:00 p.m. on weekdays. My grandmother would visit with her neighbors as they walked in front of the house on the unpaved street that was covered with miniature gravel. Often, a passing neighbor would be invited to sit on the porch with us for an extended visit. When I was in the swing alone, I sometimes would use my feet to push off making the swing go high into the air, reminding me of the swings at my school; if observed doing this, I was scolded and told that swinging so high could cause me to fall out of the swing and break my arm. The thought of going to the doctor for a broken limb was usually enough to deter me from continuing the activity for the time being.

At one end of the porch was an enclosed area, referred to as the porch room, where my grandparents stored a wringer-type washing machine, a large galvanized tub, and other supplies. I would observe Papaw carrying the galvanized tub outside to one corner of the house and placing it on the ground to catch the water from the rain that would flow from the roof. When the tub was full of water, my grandfather would carry it back to the porch room to be used later for bathing and doing laundry. A privy, just like the one at my house, was located in the back yard.

Inside the house were a living area, two small bedrooms, a kitchen and an area for bathing. The living area served as a space to listen to the radio, read, or engage in conversation. A fireplace, which Papaw called a grate box, was located in the wall that separated the living area from the largest bedroom; it opened into both rooms. A roaring fire in the grate box provided enough heat to warm most of the small dwelling. On overnight stays during the winter, I would often find myself sitting in Mamaw's lap covered by a warm blanket in the evenings, waiting for the return of Papaw from his shift at the mines. My grandmother would sing to me and tell me interesting stories of her life as a child in Roanoke, Virginia. I always looked forward to Mamaw wrapping three large potatoes in aluminum foil and placing them among the embers in the grate box. After waiting for what seemed to be forever, two of the potatoes would be removed to cool before Mamaw unwrapped the foil, placed the potatoes on a plate sliced them down the middle, and then slathered them with creamed butter. A pinch of salt and pepper was added for additional flavoring. The third potato remained in the grate box but was moved away from the hot coals and would be ready for my grandfather to enjoy when he arrived home from work.

Mamaw always had the beds made during the day, covering them with white chenille bedspreads that had beautifully colored flowers on top. I was not allowed to play on the beds after my grandmother had made them for the day. Sometimes Mamaw would allow me to jump on the bed in the morning before covering them with the bedspreads.

The kitchen area contained a sink, an electric cook stove like the one my mother used, a small refrigerator, Hoosier cabinet and a dinette set. The oval-shaped table had a yellow laminate top with shiny silver metal edging around the sides. The seats of the four chairs were covered in yellow vinyl and the legs and backs were made of chrome. The refrigerator usually housed several bottles of RC Cola, which I would receive as a special treat during my visits. Mamaw, just as my Mom, would try to coax me into a daily dosing of cod liver oil, which I always resisted unless I was promised a small portion of an RC Cola; sometimes I would pretend to take a small taste of the horrible-tasting elixir which always satisfied Mamaw enough to give me the cola.

Bath time at my grandparents' house was not something that I looked forward to during my visits. Unlike the porcelain tub at my house, Mamaw and Papaw used a long, oval-shaped galvanized tub for bathing. Mamaw would use water that she dipped from the galvanized tub in the porch room and heat it on the electric stove top until it boiled; the hot water would be transferred to the bathtub mixing with cold water already in the tub. My grandmother would always make sure that the water temperature was tepid, and not hot, before putting me in the tub.

My Mamaw, Grace Bratcher Brown, was born in Roanoke, Virginia, in 1906. Her mother had died when she was very young, leaving my great-grandfather with his four daughters. Mamaw's three sisters and her father, who was in declining health, continued to live in Roanoke and she would correspond with them often by writing letters; sometimes she would read me the letters received from her sisters that referenced places and events that were completely alien to me. Unlike my Momma Poe, Mamaw and Papaw did not have a telephone in their home.

Infrequently, my grandparents would walk to a close neighbor's house that had a telephone to make and receive calls. Mamaw was able to talk with her father and three adult children who lived in Roanoke and California at Christmas when they would call the neighbor's telephone.

Benny often joined me for overnight stays. Mamaw told us that her father had played the violin when he was younger; she referred to the stringed instrument as a "fiddle" and had talked about how she and her sisters enjoyed singing while her father accompanied them on the fiddle. Occasionally after telling us about her father, she would break out in song and Benny and I would hear:

> *Old Dan Tucker was a fine old man*
> *Washed his face with a frying pan*
> *Combed his hair with a wagon wheel*
> *And died with a toothache in his heel*
> *Get out the way, Old Dan Tucker*
> *You're too late to get your supper*
> *Get out the way, Old Dan Tucker*
> *You're too late to get your supper!*

Sometimes Benny and I would be lucky enough to witness instrumental entertainment as my grandmother would remove her French harp from its beautiful, silk-lined case and then move it back and forth across her lips, exhaling and inhaling interchangeably, to ensure that the reeds were open. The air would then be filled with the sweet musical sounds of the folk tunes *Oh, Susannah* or *Down in the Valley*.

My Papaw, Nicholas Thomas Brown, was born in Scott County, Virginia, in 1896. After an extremely limited formal education, my grandfather accompanied his father to the state of West Virginia to begin a career in coal mining that would extend until his retirement some fifty years later. Papaw's marriage to my grandmother was his second, the first union having produced two sons, both of whom were grown and only visited infrequently. I loved being picked up by my grandfather and embraced and often pleaded with him to swing me by my arms round and round.

Upon standing I would lose my balance staggering about the room and Papaw would smile while saying, "Thomas Lee, you look like a drunken man trying to walk." I did not really understand my Papaw's amusement for I never had seen a drunken man trying to walk.

I looked forward to sitting on my Papaw's knees while he would bounce me around singing *Pop Goes the Weasel.* Papaw always would hesitate after singing, "...The monkey thought 'twas all in fun..." before spreading apart his knees letting me fall to the floor before finishing with, "...Pop!—goes the weasel." Papaw seemed to never get tired of playing this game with me as he always would grant my request of begging him to do it over and over again.

Papaw wore metal-rimmed glasses that fit snugly over his ears. I often would remove the glasses from his face while sitting in his lap, place them on my face, and walk around the room. My vision was impaired by the glasses, and I would sometimes stagger about before my grandfather would remove them calling me a silly boy. I was struck by the tiny blue specks that dotted Papaw's forehead and sometimes would attempt to count them all. Mamaw had told me that the blue dots were actually tiny specks of coal that had become embedded in the skin of my grandfather's face over the course of his many years working underground in the coal mines.

I was fascinated with Papaw's mining uniform; like our neighbor, Mr. Nolan, he referred to his uniform as bank clothes. Mamaw told me that I was not to attempt to examine the bank clothes since they often were covered with black coal dust; the bank clothes, along with other mining items, were always stored on the inside porch near the washing machine. When Papaw would return home from a work shift, he would be wearing a hard, metal cap that had a light on its front. The light was powered with calcium carbide, the same element used by my Mom to ameliorate the minerals in water used for laundry. The mixture of elements would create a small white flame that was used by my grandfather as a light source when he worked underground. My favorite component of Papaw's mining gear was the metal canister with a lid that served as his dinner bucket.

I would always check his dinner bucket as soon as he arrived home to see if there was a sweet treat that he had not eaten; I think my grandfather was delighted in seeing that I never was disappointed.

I had asked Papaw about the giant bath house when I accompanied him to the post office on Saturdays and had inquired about going inside. My grandfather agreed that I could go along with him to take a shower. I was excited about the adventure as the two of us drove to the bathhouse. Papaw had told me on the way there to stay with him at all times, and that there would be some other men taking showers while we were there. When we entered the facility, I followed my grandfather to a large, open room lined with tall metal cabinets and long metal benches in the middle of the floor. The two of us disrobed, and Papaw stored our clothes in one of the cabinets. Then we walked to another large room that had several long metal pipes stretching down from the ceiling; faucets were attached to the bottom of the pipes along with a tray where Papaw placed a cake of soap that he had brought with us. The room had little resemblance to the shower in our basement; the water had to travel farther down to reach my body and made me feel like I was being pelted by the rain in a heavy storm. After lathering and rinsing our bodies, including Papaw's indulgence of allowing me to spend much more time than I needed to rinse, we returned to the room where our clothes were stored to dry off and get dressed before returning home.

Only once did my grandfather become so angry with me that he gave me a spanking. My grandmother was away from home and Debbie had accompanied me to spend a couple of days and nights with Papaw; Debbie had agreed to prepare our meals in Mamaw's absence. As we were bringing our clothes in from the car and walking up the steps to the porch, I wanted my sister to see the outside porch. While the two of us were exploring the room, I noticed my grandfather's fedora hat with the wide brim hanging from a large nail. Wanting to show off for my sister, I impetuously took the hat off the nail and threw it in the tub of water that had been collected from the rain. Shocked, Debbie exclaimed, "Oh no! Why did you do that? You are going to be in real trouble!" "I won't get in trouble with Papaw. He won't do anything to me," I replied, smiling. Debbie went inside the house and returned with my grandfather who saw his hat floating in the tub of water. "Thomas Lee, why did you throw my hat in the water? That hat cost a lot of hard-earned money and I think you've ruined it." I hung my head and offered no reply. Becoming angrier by the minute, Papaw took me by the hand walking me inside the house saying, "You are going to get a hard spanking for what you have done, little man." I was confounded for the rest of the evening while I sobbed, getting no consolation from my sister or grandfather.

Later in his mining career, my grandfather injured his back in an accident inside the mine. Papaw's age and his injury combined to cause a fairly rapid deterioration of his physical stamina. The mining company's workers' compensation insurance carrier had offered my grandfather a settlement for his back injury, which he decided to accept. My grandfather's union pension, along with Social Security benefits and the settlement payout, would be adequate to cover the family's living expenses. Papaw made his retirement from coal mining official, and he and my grandmother began to look forward to receiving the settlement payout in the mail. Papaw had promised me that he would buy me a cowboy suit that I had seen in Brock's Department Store in Harveytown. I had also requested a double holster set with two new cap guns. During my continued visits, I always asked to go along with Papaw to the post office, curious to know if the settlement check had arrived. The day the check arrived, I happened to be visiting and was lucky enough to make the trip to Harveytown with my grandparents where I received my new cowboy suit, complete with a brimmed hat and holster with cap pistols. Once I tried the new suit on, I did not want to take it off, and wore it home.

I was always leery and a little fearful of the large body of black-crusted water that was located at the lower end of Coalgap, where the colored families lived. Papaw told me it was a sludge pond containing liquid waste that was produced from the crushing and washing of coal that came from underground. The pond was located by the highway where the road banked and curved sharply, always frightening me as we would drive past. One night at my grandparents' house, I experienced a vivid dream where Papaw's car did not quite round the curve, going off the road and crashing into the sludge pond. I felt totally helpless as the vehicle sank under the water and was covered by a black, crusty canopy. I could only see black outside the car's windows and began to think my Papaw and I would drown. Awakening suddenly, I lurched out of bed telling my grandmother, with whom I was sleeping, "Help me! Are Papaw and I going to drown?" Mamaw helped me to awake fully and reassured me that everything was OK.

It was summer and my grandparents had promised me that I could accompany them to visit with family who lived on a large farm at Sandy Gap. I was told that it might take as long as two hours for Papaw to drive us there. I always became excited while traveling in a car because I would be able to see lots of new things and places. Mamaw had made a hearty breakfast before we began our journey. I watched in anticipation as she cut the frying chicken into two drumsticks, two thighs, two breasts, two wings, and back portions. The chicken was then dipped in an egg mixture, rolled in flour, and placed in a sizzling cast iron skillet holding melted hot lard. The chicken was fried until the meat was done and covered with a crisp, golden-brown coating. The lard was then drained from the skillet leaving only the crunchy morsels of breading that had fallen from the meat. Mamaw added flour, milk and a can of tomatoes to the breading to create a creamy tomato gravy that would cover the delicious homemade biscuits that were baking. The meal was served with a cold glass of sweet milk and hastily eaten in order for us to begin our trip.

The trip took us through downtown Harveytown and then on to Cedartown as the highway followed the path of the Clinch River for most of the way. We passed several large metal bridges like the one that spanned the river at Duffield just outside of Harveytown. In what seemed like more than two hours spent driving, our journey continued toward Morrisville on US 24, where we turned right before reaching the town to make our way to Sandy Gap. When we arrived at the farm, we were greeted by my grandfather's relatives, who invited us into the house. The house was large and had two floors with a large staircase leading from the first to second level. I had never been to a home with an upstairs living space in the house. I immediately wanted to explore the upstairs but resisted the urge since I was in an unfamiliar place. Everyone was invited to sit for conversation while drinks were served. Someone, whom I did not know, brought me a soda from the kitchen. The refreshing drink made me more at ease and it was not long until I asked Papaw if I could look around the house. Papaw responded, "No, let's wait a little longer," with our hostess saying almost at the same time, "Sure, you can look around our house. Would you like for me to show you around?" I nodded and the tour began. The first floor of the house had a living room, large kitchen, bedroom, bathroom with a tub, lavatory and commode and large pantry room. An old woman, who looked just like Mrs. Spicer, who had died, was sleeping in the bedroom. I ascended the stairs with anticipation and took the opportunity to look down to the first level several times, marveling at how high up I was. I saw three more bedrooms upstairs and a large closet covered by a colorful curtain. I made my way back downstairs and began to tell my grandparents about everything I had seen. As everyone continued to talk and visit, I sat quietly, imagining myself living in this big house and how much fun it would be to slide down the railing on the stairs. Benny and I could share a room upstairs and pretend to live in a clubhouse high in a tree. My imagination continued to run wild until everyone had a bathroom break and Papaw asked me if I would like to go outside with him and look around the farm.

Papaw and I walked through the yard until we reached a large fence with barbed wire on top. I saw several cows, just like those pictured in my books at school, eating the tall grass. One of the cows raised his head emitting a low-pitched "Moo" before continuing to graze the field. Papaw asked if I would like to see one of the cows up close and I quickly said, "Sure. Let's go see." The cow smelled of poop and my grandfather warned me to watch for piles of waste as we walked in the field. I petted the cow, watching it swish its long tail to its back trying to knock off several flies. We walked over to the barn where the cows would go at night and talked with a man who was milking one of them. The man asked if I would like to give it a try and at first, I was hesitant to do so. Papaw encouraged me to go ahead, and I positioned myself on a wooden stool that sat low to the ground. I was somewhat squeamish as I grasped the cow's udder in my right hand and began to squeeze; nothing happened, and I kept squeezing. The man said, "You have to pull the thing down as you squeeze it to get the milk to come out." I kept trying for a few more minutes but never managed to see any milk flow. Papaw gave it a try and was able to squeeze quite a bit of milk into the bucket. We visited the hen house and found three or four brown eggs in the straw, reminding me of the eggs Mrs. Stewart had in her basket. After eating lunch, we drove back to Coalgap, arriving well after it had gotten dark outside. I visited the privy, got ready for bed, and was soon sound asleep.

9/Travels

Soon after our visit to Sandy Gap, my grandparents decided to move to a larger house located at Flat Bottom, a short distance from their current residence. My favorite thing about the house at Flat Bottom was the bathroom; it included a porcelain tub like mine at home, a lavatory and a commode. Having an indoor commode meant no more trips to the privy, especially when I would have to go at night, using Papaw's flashlight to find my way there and back. My grandparents purchased their first television and subscribed to a cable line that provided clear reception of the channels that carried the three major networks. The house had a large living room, a large kitchen with space for a much larger dining table than the dinette set they owned, two bedrooms with closet space and a long, covered front porch; a screened-in back porch housed a galvanized tub and the wringer-type washer. Papaw was especially excited that the property had a garage where he could park his car and store all his tools. There was a large front lawn and ample space for a vegetable garden behind the house. The house was heated by a relatively new *Warm Morning* coal-fired stove equipped with a blower that would allow the heat produced to be transferred quickly throughout the house. My grandparents were thrilled to live in their newer-model house with conveniences to which they previously had not been accustomed. My entire family and I were excited for them and would visit as often as my Dad was available to take us there.

Saturday nights were informally reserved as the time our entire family would travel from Dawson to Flat Bottom to visit my grandparents and watch television. Since the television provided access to broadcasts from all three networks, more selection of programming was available. Papaw would begin the evening with his eyes glued to the screen as championship wrestling was broadcast live from a venue in Knoxville, Tennessee; he loved to participate vicariously by cheering his favorites and shouting, "Get him! That's it! Put his head in a lock hold!" Mom and Dad weren't as interested in watching wrestling but would humor my Pawpaw and appear to be enjoying it; they often would tell each other privately that they were more entertained by watching my grandfather's zestful animation during the broadcast rather than the wrestling program. *Perry Mason* followed the wrestling show, bringing a host of characters who lived their lives much different from my own. I found myself totally engrossed in the suspense and drama of the show each week and looked forward to Perry exposing the criminal at the end; however, I was quite frightened of Lt. Tragg's face and voice and hoped that I would never do anything so bad that he would come after me.

The capstone to our family's evening of entertainment was watching *Gunsmoke*. My grandmother often would roast garlic wieners in the oven along with toasting slices of bread with a pat of butter. The delicious smells from the kitchen would waft into the living room, competing with the enjoyment of the television show. One Saturday night just as *Bonanza* was beginning to air, a transformer on the utility pole located across the street from the house caught fire.

Bonanza always began with the Cartwrights riding their horses through an old parchment that appeared to be on fire with the paper burning to the edges of the television. Unbeknownst to any of us watching television, the transformer blew and caught fire just as the show was beginning and it appeared that an actual fire was in the television and had consumed the Cartwright family before the screen went dark. It wasn't until Dad looked out the window and saw the actual fire on the utility pole that I could be assured by him that the Cartwrights had not been harmed.

Dad, Benny and I would return to Flat Bottom on most Sundays to continue visiting and watching television. My father's main interest was in watching NFL games that aired in the early afternoon. Sometimes we would arrive as my grandfather was watching NBC's *Meet the Press*; he and Dad would frequently debate national and international policy and political issues. Dad was a registered Republican, and both of his parents were registered, dyed-in-the-wool Democrats. Papaw had been involved with the early union organizing in Roane County and remained active in the UMWA (United Mine Workers of America) in retirement, serving as an officer in a local affiliate. One Sunday the argument got so heated with flared tempers that Dad decided that we would suspend our visit and return home. Benny and I were saddened on the way home because we didn't like hearing the people we loved fuss and argue with one another; truth be told, we were equally disappointed that we would be deprived of watching three of our favorite television programs after NFL football ended.

We wouldn't stay away from our grandparents' house very long, however, since the television programming was too much of a draw. Dad and Papaw would always reconcile and agree that they had opposing views that didn't always need to be discussed. Benny and I were always happy to again be watching *Lassie*, then *Dennis the Menace*, and finally *The Wonderful World of Disney*.

I liked to quiz each of my grandparents about shows they watched on television while I was visiting. We often made a game out of the queries by trying to guess favorites that aired on different nights. Mamaw told me that her all-time favorite show on television was *I Love Lucy*, starring Lucille Ball. Papaw loved to tell me about the re-run episodes of *Highway Patrol* he watched, starring Broderick Crawford.

Having maintained an interest in things that moved since Benny and I first began playing with toy cars and trucks, I was intrigued when I first saw a large, black and brown bus traveling on the highway in front of my grandparents' house periodically throughout the day. The bus looked quite different from the school bus that I had ridden home from Creekside School and covered the same route as the one that stopped in Dawson, taking my neighbors to Harveytown and returning them home. Papaw told me that the bus was operated by the SVTC Lines located in Bristol. The SVTC bus sometimes would stop to pick up or drop off my grandparents' neighbors; I was fascinated with the pneumatic, accordion-style door panels that folded to each side after the coach made a loud hissing noise. Unlike a school bus, the coach had two sets of doors with one located in the front opposite the driver and the other closer to the rear. My grandparents' neighbors would always enter or leave the bus through the door at the front.

I had begged Mamaw and Papaw to take me for a ride on the SVTC bus for several weeks when my grandfather announced that he would be taking the coach to town in the afternoon. My grandfather's car had been unreliable for the last week or so and he was waiting for a mechanic in the community to come see about the vehicle. I was thrilled with anticipation and excitement as we waited by the driveway for the big bus to stop for us. Remaining curious with respect to why passengers did not enter or leave from the door in the back, I asked Papaw if we could board the bus from the rear. Shaking his head "No," Papaw told me that it would be best for us to board from the front door. When the bus arrived, I persisted in wanting to enter from the rear, taking my grandfather's hand and pulling him toward the door; he initially resisted but then relented and we boarded from the rear door. There was a large bench seat in the very back of the bus; breaking loose from my grandfather, I quickly made my way there to be seated. Papaw remained standing and tried his best to coax me to sit in a seat closer to the front of the bus. Stubbornly, I remained seated and Papaw made his way back to join me. The bus would stop when someone pulled a cord above the seats that made a loud buzzing noise to signal that a passenger wanted to exit the bus. The bus stopped at Harveytown Hospital and a colored lady got on through the rear door that I had entered and sat at a seat near my grandfather and me. The lady smiled at me and both Papaw and I greeted her with, "Hello." Soon the bus arrived at the terminal building in Harveytown and all the passengers exited. The colored lady and my grandfather and I left the bus through the rear door while other passengers used the one in the front.

While walking in town, I asked, "Papaw, why did most of the passengers want to sit in the front of the bus?" He explained that the rear door and seats were for the colored people to use and that the two of us were not supposed to sit in that area. I continued to pepper my grandfather with questions, wanting to know why the two of us were supposed to sit in the front of the bus and only colored people could use the back door and enjoy the big bench seat in the rear most part of the coach; he remained equivocal and offered no plausible explanation other than, "That's just the way it is...." I knew I did not like the perplexing rule and would try to find out why it was in place.

After Papaw completed his business, we visited the J.J. Newberry store. The store was massive to my young eyes and sold a variety of merchandise. A clothing shop was in the lower section of the store that was level with the street; the upper section housed a long diner counter and a large area stocked fully with toys and books for children. I immediately guided my grandfather to the toy department and began to scan the shelves for a new toy. After buying a toy, we sat on a stool at the diner counter that was decorated with small, colorful posters of such treats as ice cream sundaes, hamburgers and French fries and grilled cheese sandwiches. Papaw ordered a hamburger for himself and French fries for me; they were served with a red plastic container of ketchup; Papaw showed me how to get the ketchup out by squeezing the bottle deftly with my hands. After we finished our meal, we walked over to a long trail of cabinets on a counter covered with glass fronts. The cabinets contained different kinds of chocolate candy and a large assortment of nuts. My grandfather bought a dime bag of peanuts for himself and a nickel's worth of chocolate-covered peanuts for me.

While waiting in the lobby of the SVTC bus terminal to return to Flat Bottom, I read a sign that said "No Colored" on a door leading into a separate room. Papaw told me that the door led into a small restaurant and that colored people had a separate door that they would use if they wanted to get something from the restaurant to take home and eat. I became even more confused, asking more questions of my grandfather that he didn't want to answer; instead, he took me to a bathroom in the rear of the room. Papaw had to put a dime in a metal slot and turn a silver knob to open a small wooden door to gain entrance to the space where a commode was located. I asked my grandfather what one would do if they needed to use the bathroom really bad and did not have a dime. Looking puzzled, he told me he did not know and that they would probably have to wait until they got home. It seemed that there were more and more things that I did not understand and could not get anyone to explain to me.

While riding the bus on another occasion, I had taken note of a sign that was posted above the driver's name that read: Safe and Sober Transportation. Papaw had explained to me that it meant the bus driver could be trusted. During today's bus ride into town, I noticed that the driver frequently slowed the bus down while traveling on the highway. Mamaw and Papaw looked concerned and discussed whether or not something was wrong. Not far outside of Harveytown, a police car with a flashing light pulled behind the bus and the driver moved the vehicle to the curb, bringing it to a complete stop. The police officer asked the driver to step outside the bus; we all now knew for sure that something was wrong. Several minutes later we watched as the police officer directed the driver to the back seat of his patrol car. Then the officer came on the bus to announce that the driver was drunk and would not be driving the bus any farther. My grandparents, along with the other passengers, shook their heads in disbelief. Shortly thereafter, a new driver arrived and drove the bus to the terminal building.

I never grew tired of visiting my grandparents, even as I aged. The summer after I completed fourth grade, Papaw took me along to fish the Roane Fork River located within walking distance of his house. We dug in the garden for fat earthworms, which I placed in an old tin can filled partially with dirt. I helped my grandfather carry the bamboo cane poles and metal tackle box to the river's bank where we would fish. Papaw attached a line and a hook to my pole and placed a large earthworm on the end of the hook. Then I dipped the hook into the river, waiting for a fish to bite. I waited and waited, but nothing happened. Papaw told me that I needed to have patience, which translated to me as standing still for even longer. After fifteen minutes or so and no fish to be seen, I asked if I could play in the shallow part of the river instead of fishing. Papaw agreed, so I removed my sneakers and began walking near the river's edge. My grandfather continued to fish for another forty-five minutes with no luck either before we headed on home.

Shortly after 9:00 p.m. one evening while watching television with Papaw, I became very hungry. I told Mamaw and she offered to prepare me a sandwich. However, a sandwich just didn't seem appetizing to me; my mind was fantasizing about how great a fried chicken basket from a drive-in restaurant would taste. I asked Papaw if he would take me to get the chicken basket and he first said, "No, it's too late to be out. Your Mamaw will give you something to eat here if you're that hungry." In that I felt more famished than ever, I continued to nag Papaw. Mamaw told him, "You have no business going out this late. Thomas Lee can eat something here." When I began to tear up, Papaw got up from the couch and went into the bedroom to get his shoes, wallet and car keys. Mamaw was standing in the doorway shaking her head in disbelief as we pulled out of the driveway. I savored every bite of the fried chicken and French fries, giving Papaw the chicken pieces that I did not eat.

My infatuation with buses did not wane and I kept looking for a toy bus at J.J. Newberry on trips to town with my grandparents. Mamaw had told me that she would buy a toy bus for me if we saw one on a shopping trip and I had not forgotten the promise. Using his ingenuity, Papaw had made a toy bus from a shoe box by using his pocketknife to cut out windows just like the ones on the SVTC bus; he even made front and rear doors that would open and close by cutting the box on three sides of the rectangle and leaving the fourth side to fold in and out. I would move the box over the wooden floors pretending that I was driving an SVTC bus. I strategically placed plastic toy soldiers in different parts of the room stopping to move them into the bus through the doors and continuing my journey. I even had a pretend terminal building where all the passengers disembarked and embarked.

My grandparents were planning a trip to Roanoke to visit relatives and I begged them to go along; the two of them agreed that I could go if Mom and Dad would give permission. Fervently, I pleaded with my parents to be allowed to make the trip and after much deliberation, permission was granted. Mamaw brought out of the closet a suitcase that had been given to her by her daughter. Mom had assembled my clothes and other personal items that I would need, and they were carefully packed along with all my grandparents' clothing and toiletries. My Dad drove us to the Greyhound bus station in Harveytown where Papaw purchased our tickets while Mamaw and I waited in the lobby. When the dispatcher announced that the bus we would take had arrived and was ready for boarding, I became even more excited about going on the coach for a long trip. The Greyhound bus looked much newer than the SVTC bus and had two large spaces on its side for passengers' luggage. I immediately observed that unlike the SVTC bus, the Greyhound coach only had one door located at the front of the vehicle. The three of us boarded the bus and soon were on our way. Just as I had observed when I traveled to the farm at Sand Gap, the highway seemed to run parallel with the river for most of the way to Cedartown. The bus stopped in Cedartown and then in Morrisville when more passengers boarded. We crossed a very high mountain before arriving in Carter's Mill; as the driver maneuvered the bus through all the switch-backs, Papaw told me that we were traveling on Wise Mountain. The bus station in Carter's Mill was much larger than any of the others I had seen, with a few passengers leaving the bus and several other people boarding.

The driver continued toward Roanoke stopping at Ducan, Mountain View, Flat Lick, and Raidertown. After several hours, we arrived in Roanoke and exited the bus to go inside the terminal building. The bathrooms in the Roanoke terminal did not require a dime to gain entrance like those in Harveytown and had more commodes than I had ever seen. The men's bathroom also had a wall where several huge, porcelain covered bowls were attached that Papaw and I used to pee. Papaw called them urinals and using them reminded me of relieving myself behind the privy on occasion when it was occupied, and I could not wait.

We rode in a taxi from the bus station to my grandfather's sister's house where we were staying. The house had an upstairs and I was shown a small room there that had a window that looked out onto the back lawn. We had dinner and watched a television program before retiring to bed. I had no trouble falling asleep since the bus ride had tired me out.

We were up very early the next morning to eat breakfast, and then rode across town to visit Mamaw's father and sisters. Her sisters had traveled to her father's house prior to our arrival. I was introduced to my great-grandfather, who had gray hair and a long gray beard; he was wearing coveralls and appeared to have difficulty moving about even when aided by his cane. The man had a low, gruff voice and I was afraid of him. Mamaw tried to get me to sit in my great-grandfather's lap, but I refused to do so. We continued visiting for two or three hours before leaving.

On the third day of our visit, we took a taxi to downtown Roanoke to shop. We visited a large department store that had an escalator and an elevator, neither of which I had ever seen before. I could not take my eyes off the escalator, where the steps kept disappearing at the top, and rode it repeatedly until Papaw became tired. Mamaw bought a bag of candy at the store which she shared among the three of us.

As we were waiting in the lobby of the Roanoke bus station for our return trip, I spotted a large assortment of toys hanging on a metal carousel. Mamaw told me it was OK to walk over to look and I did just that. As I turned the carousel, I saw bags of plastic toy soldiers, colored pencils, toy cars, toy dishes and toy make-up bags along with many other items. Suddenly, I spotted a long, colorful box wrapped in plastic that had a picture of a Greyhound bus just like the one I had ridden to Roanoke. I ran over to tell my grandmother what I had seen and asked her to come look at the toy. Mamaw examined the package and told me that there was a toy Greyhound bus inside the box; I reminded her that she had promised to buy a bus for me and after checking the price, she took the toy bus to a counter to purchase the item. I ran back to my seat with the toy and opened the package, removing a small replica of an actual Greyhound bus. The coach's door would open and close and when I moved the bus along the floor, the realistic-like wheels rolled making a hissing noise. I was so happy that I Momentarily left my bus on the floor and hugged my grandmother tightly thanking her over and over.

My grandparents moved from Flat Bottom to a house in Harveytown when I was in fourth grade. Mamaw told me that because of their ages, they wanted to be closer to town where more conveniences were available. Our family continued to visit but not as frequently and Benny and I still spent the night on occasion. Dad had gotten the picture tube in our television at home replaced, rather than purchasing a new set, and the reception had somewhat improved. I would often suggest to Mom and Dad that we visit my grandparents to watch television and they would remind me that we had a television at home. I spent the night with my grandparents the weekend after President Kennedy had been assassinated. My television programming lineup for Saturday morning had been preempted by coverage of Lee Harvey Oswald's transfer from the Dallas police building to a more secure jail. The three of us were watching the television when a man walked up and shot Oswald. I immediately knew that what I had seen was real and that I could not compare it in my mind with what I had seen on *Bonanza* or *Perry Mason*. "Was Oswald dead?" I thought. "Will the police catch the man who shot Oswald and not let him get away? Will the man shoot other people?" I contemplated. I could see the expressions on my grandparents' faces knowing that they were feeling as disturbed as I. Mamaw suggested that I may want to call my parents and talk with them about what I had seen which I did.

During the fall of 1964, I found myself longing to visit my grandparents more than I ever had before. I felt empty inside and seeing my Mamaw and Papaw seemed to be the right medicine to make the pain and loneliness go away for a time. Both Benny and I were older now and had developed interests beyond watching television and playing cars and trucks. Our grandparents regularly provided us with monetary gifts during our visits and we wasted no time in making our way into Harveytown to spend them.

We had first been introduced to board games when our father purchased *Monopoly* and brought the game home for our family to enjoy. Benny and I sometimes pooled our money in order to purchase games such as *Mousetrap* and *Life*. Papaw had developed an interest in playing cards, especially solitaire, and he often could be observed cheating at the game crowing, "I beat old Sol!" Mamaw would join us to play *Rook* as a substitute for watching television during the daylight hours.

In the late 1960s, Sears, Roebuck and Company opened a small store in Harveytown near the Dawson Hospital. The hospital had undergone a name change and was now Southwest Virginia Regional Hospital. The store stocked a few of the items offered in the company's catalog but its primary draw was the acceptance of catalog orders that would arrive at the store for pick-up only a few days later. A friend's parents had gotten him a *Mattel Thing Maker* at the Sears store, and I wanted one of my own. Papaw drove me out to the store and placed the order for the toy and returned to pick it up for me a few days later. I quickly learned to avoid touching the hot metal molds and heating surface while making my slimy plastic bugs.

I was now old enough for my grandparents to feel comfortable with allowing me to walk from their house to a public swimming pool operated by the city of Harveytown. The walk was a mile away but easily traversed by using the sidewalks. After paying my admission, I would check out a wire basket to store my belongings while I changed into swim trunks. The pool was always crowded with teenagers and younger kids alike, with lounge chairs lined around its sides. I taught myself to swim at the pool by first going underwater in the shallow end and then braving the deeper waters where the diving board was located. I learned to love the water and would ask to visit the pool during my visits with Mamaw and Papaw as weather would allow.

Benny and I had taken boat rides on Lonesome Creek Lake with our neighbors, the Youngs. While fishing, I had seen several people in very small canoes on the water and it captured my imagination. My opportunity arrived when I spotted an inflatable canoe made of plastic for sale in one of the stores in Harveytown while visiting my grandparents. The price of the item was more money than I had available at the time, so I decided to save my money until I had enough to purchase the canoe. I bought the canoe during a weekend visit and couldn't wait to get home and try it out. I told Benny of my plans for testing the canoe in water, hoping he would join me; he wasn't at all keen on the idea and didn't seem to think my plan would work. I walked up the street a mile or so from our house carrying the deflated canoe. Once I arrived at a place where I had walking access to the creek that ran out of the hollow, I inflated the canoe with my breath. It took me fifteen minutes or so to blow the boat up. I had noticed that the level of water in the creek had risen and was flowing more quickly than usual due to the rain we had received the day before. My plan was to put the canoe into the shallow water in order to board it and then ride it down to the bottom of the hill located a mile or so away from where I was standing. I summoned my courage and boarded the boat, pushing off into the water with my hands. The boat traveled slowly at first but then picked up speed as it made its way toward the bottom of the hill. I was having a lot of fun and my plan was working until I encountered water that was much more turbulent. The canoe began to tilt from side to side and I was having a difficult time controlling it. Suddenly, the canoe hit a rock and I toppled out with my transport continuing without me. Soaking wet, I watched forlornly as the canoe rapidly moved farther away from my line of sight; I realized that I would not be riding it again. I returned home and told Benny about what had happened, and he suggested we go to the bottom of the hill to look for the boat that may have washed ashore; we did so but there was no canoe to be found. Walking back home I kept thinking about how much fun I had riding the canoe down the creek even though I had spent a lot of my money on the purchase and would not see the boat again.

My visits to Mamaw and Papaw's house seldom included an overnight stay after 1967. I still relished my time with them and called them on the telephone to talk fairly regularly. When I did spend the night, I still enjoyed sleeping in a featherbed with Mamaw's red rubber hot water bottle for extra warmth and falling asleep thinking about the delicious breakfast I would be eating the next morning.

10/Christmas

My family began preparing for Christmas two weeks or so ahead of the much-anticipated day. It seemed that everyone was in a good mood and that I would have minor misbehavior overlooked by Mom and Dad. As we kids were teeming with excitement and enjoying lively conversations about presents we hoped for, our mother would always remind us of the true reason for the holiday season: the birth of the Christ Child.

My older brothers and sister were entrusted with foraging the mountains above our house for the perfect red cedar tree that would make its way into our living room. Johnny and Ronnie were allowed to carry two of Dad's hatchets that he used on scouting expeditions to chop down the tree. When the three of them returned with our Christmas tree in 1963, they were not smiling and as jovial as I had remembered them being in past years. I went outside with Mom to greet my siblings and examine the green, sweet-smelling branches and listened as Johnny told the story of locating the beautiful tree high on the hill in a thicket where several identical conifers were growing. After the tree had been chopped down, the three of them heard a loud voice shouting from the bottom of the hill, which was a considerable distance from where they were standing. Johnny had made his way out of the thicket when he saw a man with a shotgun standing below him. The man had demanded, "Who are you? Don't you know this is my property? Did you cut down one of my trees?" Johnny noted he had apologized to the man, telling him that he and his brother had cut down the tree for Christmas and that they didn't know it belonged to him. Johnny said he offered to leave the tree as it was on the ground, but the man told him that he could go ahead and take it but to not return to his property. Mom apologized to everyone for what had occurred and said that we would find a Christmas tree next year in the mountains near Momma Poe's house.

Johnny trimmed off some of the lower branches from the tree to expose the trunk while Mom located a pail and filled it half full of water. Both the pail and the tree were carried into the house to the living room and the tree trunk was secured in the pail with rocks. Later that evening, a large box was removed from the closet shelf in Debbie's bedroom and placed on the living room floor. We all participated as shiny glass ornaments were carefully taken from the box to be examined and admired. Dad untangled the strands of red, blue, green, yellow, and white lights, telling us that they needed to go on the tree before we could hang the ornaments. One strand of the lights would not work, and my father explained that the bulb sockets were wired in a series and if a single bulb had burned out, the entire strand would not light. I didn't understand any of what Dad had explained and was growing impatient with him spending so much time trying to locate the faulty bulb. After an hour or so, Dad had all the strands working and had begun to string them around the tree. My favorite strand of lights was the one that would produce tiny bubbles in a small glass tube; I would watch them, mesmerized, as my eyes moved from one to another.

I was excited when I looked at the lights glowing on the Christmas tree after the strands were plugged into the electrical socket. It was time to hang the ornaments! It was Mom containing my zest this time saying, "We can't put the ornaments on yet. I need to drape the garland first." I watched as my mother took a long rope of gold tinsel and scalloped it around the beautiful tree; the tinsel sparkled in the glow of the lights.

Finally, everyone was given the go-ahead to hang the beautiful ornaments throughout the tree. Debbie advised that we shouldn't hang very many ornaments on the back of the tree since it was positioned against the wall, and no one could see them. Just like the tinsel, the glass ornaments were reflected by the lights on the tree and were beautiful to behold. Ronnie opened a box of tinsel icicles that everyone draped over the branches of the tree before the final decoration was added. A star, covered with tinsel, was removed from the bottom of the box and placed on the apex of the topmost branch of the tree. Mom told us that the star reminded her of the Star of Bethlehem that guided The Three Wise Men to the Christ Child. An old white sheet wrapped around the bottom of the tree to conceal the pail of water completed the decoration that would focus our family's attention on a special day to be celebrated very soon.

The older kids would make a second trip to the mountains, this time visiting the hilly terrain near Grandma Poe's house, to look for greenery to decorate other places in our house. Debbie told me that female holly branches with red berries were very hard to find in the densely-forested mountains. My older brothers also looked each year for mistletoe that could be found growing high in the branches of some trees. Sometimes, finding pinecones that had fallen to the ground added a little serendipity to the expedition. The holly branches that were found would be placed on tabletops and often were accented with red candles. Glue drops were applied to the pinecones before they were sprinkled with school glitter and strung on a colorful ribbon for hanging. Although my brothers searched for the mistletoe each year, none ever was found.

Small pieces of hard candy, some of which had a soft, sweet center, were placed in decorative dishes for everyone's enjoyment on Christmas Eve. Peppermint candy canes that my mother had purchased on a grocery shopping trip to further decorate the Christmas tree had a way of disappearing from the tree's branches well before Christmas. Mom and Dad enjoyed the loaf-shaped fruitcake from the A&P store; this Christmas treat seemed to last for quite a while in the kitchen since none of us kids would eat it.

Music played a large role in enriching the lives of my family, especially at Christmas. My father played the piano by ear, having taught himself on a used, upright console that was in a corner of our living room until Mom decided that it was consuming too much space. From time to time, I would sit at the piano exploring the keyboard, listening keenly to the variation in tones that could be produced by depressing different keys. Dad had told me that the piano's keys were covered with ivory taken from the tusks of elephants. I did not want to think very long about the elephants I had seen in my schoolbooks having their tusks cut off to make piano keys.

Before the piano was removed, Dad would sometimes play the tunes of carols at Christmastime. The family would sing the familiar carols of *Silent Night, Jingle Bells,* and *Rudolph the Red-nosed Reindeer* as we enjoyed the company of one another. One night while Dad and I were returning from an evening of watching television at my grandparents' house, my father asked if we wanted to sing carols to pass the time during the trip. I responded, "Yes!" and joined in with Dad singing songs I knew from memory. After singing *Rudolph the Red-nosed Reindeer,* Dad offered to teach me a new, funny verse of the song that he thought I would like:

> *Deadeye the one-eyed cowboy,*
> *Had a very shiny gun.*
> *And if you ever saw it,*
> *You would take off and run.*
> *All of the other cowboys,*
> *Used to laugh and call him names.*
> *They wouldn't let poor Deadeye,*
> *Join in any cowboy game.*
> *Then one foggy Christmas Eve,*
> *The sheriff came to say.*
> *Deadeye with your gun so bright,*
> *Won't you ride with me tonight?*
> *Then all the other cowboys,*
> *How they shouted out with glee.*
> *Deadeye the one-eyed cowboy,*
> *You'll go down in history.*

Just as the parody ended, Dad slammed on the brakes of the car and steered it to the side of the road. I exclaimed, "Did we wreck the car? Did another car hit us?" Dad regained his composure and reassured me that we had not been in an accident but that instead, the headlights on the car had gone out. Dad spent several minutes checking a fuse in the car before getting the lights to work and driving us home safely.

Christmas programs airing on the television at home and at my grandparents' meant that many of my favorite shows would be preempted which didn't always set well with me. Most, if not all, of the Christmas shows were filled with music and lasted a full hour. I did enjoy *Alvin and the Chipmunks* Christmas specials as much as I loved to watch Alvin, Theodore and Simon throughout the year; I continued to watch re-runs of the original animated series well into the late 1960s. *A Charlie Brown Christmas* was watched and enjoyed by my entire family. For some unknown reasons, my grandfather detested Perry Como and would always leave the room when he appeared on television singing in a Christmas variety show.

One really cold night on Christmas Eve, our whole family was in the living room, staying close to the coal stove. A knock was heard at the door leading to our front porch; Dad answered the door and instead of inviting someone in, stepped outside himself. After a few minutes, my father returned inside accompanied by Santa Claus, who asked if there were boys in the house. Benny and I leapt up from our nest on the floor to greet Santa. Santa looked at me and asked, "Have you been a good boy this year?" I quickly nodded, "Yes," while Johnny and Ronnie called out in unison, "No, he has not!" My brothers were corrected quickly as I told Santa, "I have so been a good boy! Just ask my Mom and Dad." Mom and Dad both assured Santa that Benny and I had been good boys and he reached into his sack and gave each of us a sucker before leaving. I could not believe that Santa Claus had been in my house but was confused that he came early and did not leave any presents. I overheard Mom telling Dad that Santa Claus was really Mr. Hatfield, our neighbor, who probably was drunk since she could smell alcohol on him.

The Christmas stocking that I put out for Santa to fill with goodies was an old sock that my Dad no longer wore. Since we didn't have a fireplace, I carefully placed the sock over the back of a chair in the living room that sat close to the stove. I often wondered how a fat Santa Claus would be able to come down such a small opening in the stove pipe that extended to a brick chimney on our roof. Moreover, I couldn't understand how the man could keep from being severely burned or even killed crashing into the hot coals in the belly of the stove. I would check my sock on Christmas morning, always finding it filled with an orange or tangerine, an apple, nuts and several delicious chocolate drops.

Christmas activities began earlier at school than they did at our house. My teachers would bring a tree from home and position it at the front of the room for everyone to see throughout the school day. There were no lights on the Christmas trees at school; instead, we children would make long paper chains using strips of colorful construction paper and paste. I liked to color the stars that would be cut from paper before being hung with paper clips on the branches of the tree. Just like our tree at home, the top of the tree at school would be decorated with a giant star, usually made by the teacher using yellow construction paper and glitter.

The bulletin boards in our classrooms would be transformed from containing word strips and multiplication tables to becoming colorful displays for Christmas scenes. Sometimes I could not stop looking at Santa Claus and his reindeer pulling a big red sleigh. A large bag of toys would be resting on the sleigh next to Santa and long strips of cotton batting would be on the bottom of the bulletin board, resembling an actual bank of deep snow. In the mid-1960s, one of my teachers had a bulletin board with a three-dimensional snowman displayed that had been made by cutting large Styrofoam balls in half and decorating them with eyes, a mouth and a nose, and a black belt and a hat. Almost all my teachers displayed a crèche in some form.

Special books with Christmas themes would be brought out by both my classroom teachers and the librarian. Every kid loved to hear the teacher read, *'Twas the Night before Christmas and The Littlest Angel'*. Prior to Christmas vacation from school, traditional carols would replace songs from the music book. I looked forward each year to my teachers borrowing a record player from the school's library and playing Christmas-themed records. Mrs. Golden always played *On the Good Ship Lollipop*, along with Christmas records, since everyone requested to hear it so we could dream of all the sweet Christmas treats we soon would eat.

The school cafeterias prepared a special Christmas lunch that was looked forward to by kids and teachers alike. Turkey and dressing with gravy, mashed potatoes, green beans and freshly-baked dinner rolls were served along with a small carton of milk. The special dessert of red velvet cake was sometimes eaten first because I so looked forward to its taste in my mouth washed down with a swig of milk.

Several weeks before the start of Christmas vacation, everyone would be asked to bring a note from their parents giving permission for drawing the name of a classmate for whom a Christmas present would be bought. I always felt sad for the kids, of whom there were few, whose parents wouldn't consent for them to participate in the name drawing. I did observe over the years that the teacher always brought a Christmas present for classmates that did not participate in the drawing activity. Most of my teachers placed a limit of twenty-five cents on the amount of money to be spent on a gift. Most of my classmates and I received presents of crayons and a coloring book, a story book, or a box of cherry cordials. As the presents were opened, I would wish for a box of the cherry cordials since I enjoyed eating the candy and knew that I only saw it in the stores at Christmastime. If I received a coloring book and crayons, there would usually be a classmate that received cherry cordials who really had wanted a different present and readily would agree to trade with me.

My church, for obvious reasons, extended the Christmas season from shortly after Thanksgiving until after New Year's Day. On the Sunday before Christmas, every kid would receive a treat bag from the church containing an apple, orange, tangerine, several English walnuts, a package of peanuts, a candy bar, several pieces of hard candy and fifty cents. The bags would not be distributed until the morning service had ended and people were leaving the building. I had trouble paying attention to the minister during the service since the treat bags to be distributed had been stacked on a large table in the back of the church and could be seen by a quick turn of the head.

Each year, the children at the church would perform in a Christmas play that would include a Nativity scene. Mary would be draped in a sheet and Joseph would be wearing a bath robe. Shepherds would wear pillowcases covering the tops of their head that were secured with a small, braided rope along with bath robes. The Three Wise Men would wear fancy hats with jewelry attached and colorful coats. The youth director and others would construct a realistic-looking stable on the stage of the church using two-by-four boards, cardboard, and actual hay strewn about the floor.

On one night, Billy was playing the role of a wise man and was taking his assignment quite seriously. I was dressed as a shepherd along with two of my close friends. As the Christmas story scripture was being read, one of my friends began to tickle Billy behind the ear with a piece of straw. At first, Billy ignored the irritation; when it occurred again, Billy quickly turned around and asked with an angry whisper, "Who did that? You better stop it!" When my friend tickled Billy's ear a third time, he stood up and shouted, "If someone doesn't make these boys leave me alone, I'll tear this whole damn thing down!" A thunderous roar of laughter could be heard throughout the sanctuary and the play ended abruptly.

Both adults and children at the church always were invited to participate in caroling on Christmas night. Sometimes I would go along just for the adventure of seeing all the neighbors come onto their porches to greet us revelers. Often, leftover Christmas treats, such as cookies and fudge, would be offered to us by the neighbors. Before the singing began, everyone would light the wick of a candle that would send a sea of warm glow to those whom we visited.

Despite Mom's best effort to keep us kids focused on the sacred meaning of the Christmas season, the never-ending thoughts of new toys and other presents made it an arduous task each and every day; the struggle was exacerbated for me the last two or three days before Christmas as I was constantly focused on the one special gift that I had asked Santa to bring. When the *Sears, Roebuck Christmas Wish book* catalog would come in the mail, my siblings and I would argue and debate over who would be the first to examine page after page of toys and other items shown in the thick compendium. Mom and Dad allowed us to write in the catalog, which I availed myself of the opportunity to do. I would draw a big circle around those items I wished to receive as Christmas presents knowing that it was certain that all of them would not be arriving at our house. Sometimes, Ronnie,

Benny and I would circle several of the same toys, which I hoped would improve my chances of receiving the item, even if it meant sharing with one of my brothers.

My dreaming about presents would be reinforced throughout the month of December as I always wanted to accompany my mother on her shopping trips to the A&P store in Harveytown. The large shelves along the walls would be loaded with toys of every kind. I would spend my entire time in the store walking back and forth closely examining each and every toy hoping that some of them would be tucked away in Santa's sleigh for me. When I learned (and reluctantly accepted) that my parents bought the toys and other presents and brought them to my house, instead of Santa Claus, I did not stop wanting to visit the grocery store before Christmas; I did, however, begin to take note of the prices since I knew my parents had a limited budget.

Trips to Harveytown before Christmas with Mamaw and Papaw always included stops at the JJ Newberry store. The department seemed to have twice as many items as compared to what I had seen during other visits throughout the year. Box after box of toy trucks and trains were stacked on top of one another. Bicycles were assembled and displayed not only in the toy department but throughout the store. I almost always would watch as my grandparents purchased my favorite toy. Then they would tell me that I couldn't play with it until Christmas, which was both disappointing and confusing. During most Christmas seasons, my manipulative strategy of begging and pleading, sometimes even pretending to cry, led to the toy coming out of the box well before Christmas.

A couple of weeks before Christmas in 1962, I was riding into town with my father to pick up something for Mamaw and Papaw. As we drove past a beautiful, two-story, brick-colonial home, I saw something out the window of the car that caused me to scream, "Slow down, Dad! Please stop!" A boy, who appeared to be about my age, was riding in a miniature car that was moving up the long driveway; a man was standing near the boy, smiling as he watched. "Dad, is that a real car that kid is driving?" I asked. My father explained to me that it was a toy car operated by a battery inside. "I'm asking Santa Claus to bring me a car like that for Christmas!" I exclaimed. Dad was silent for a few minutes before telling me that he did not think that Santa would be bringing a car to me, and that a family with a lot of money lived in the big house. I did not understand what a family having a lot of money had to do with me wanting Santa to bring me a toy car that I could drive on the street. As I continued to query my father about my request for the toy car, Dad remained evasive and changed the subject of our conversation several times before we arrived in town.

Driving through the streets of Harveytown, I noticed large ropes of decorative tinsel connected to the tall posts supporting the streetlights and spanning fully across the street from one side to the other. In the center of the rope was a large red bell illuminated by a light inside. The streets would come alive each year as the local town would sponsor an annual Christmas parade. If Dad was not available to take the family to the parade, Mamaw and Papaw would pick us up after school and drive us to town to witness the big event. The local high school bands marched in the parade, playing lively Christmas carols. Christmas-themed floats, that Dad said were made by stuffing lots of Kleenex tissues into the hexagonally-shaped holes in chicken wire that was stretched over lumber, rolled down the street. The highlight of the parade was seeing Santa Claus riding atop a shiny red fire truck and hoping to gather some of the candy pieces he tossed on the street.

After the parade had ended, I enjoyed walking up and down the sidewalks of town looking at the beautiful displays in all the store windows. JJ Newberry would dedicate at least one store window to an enchanting display of every toy imaginable. My older siblings, if they were along, liked to peruse the windows of Levine's Clothing and Watsons where fashionable clothing was on display. My very favorite window to see was at a furniture store where an animated display of elves performing acrobatic acts on a swinging ladder took place; often it would be difficult to get a peek of the displays due to the crowded sidewalks.

In 1963, Benny and I had ridden into town with our father to check on a scouting-related matter. Shortly outside of Harveytown, Dad stopped for gas at Henry Williams' Texaco service station. I looked forward to the fueling stop because I could see Mr. Williams dressed in a jacket and peaked cap with the red Texaco star in the center just like the man I would see advertising Texaco gasoline on television. This morning's stop would be different from any before, as my eyes were drawn to a large sign on display by the pump. The sign said that a new Texaco toy fire engine could be purchased for $3.98, when one would buy Sky Chief gasoline, Havoline motor oil, or Texaco anti-freeze. The picture displayed a bright red replica of an actual fire engine complete with removable ladders on the sides, removable hoses, and a red light on top. What excited me most was learning that the toy truck's hoses could be connected to a water hose and that real water would shoot out of a large silver nozzle located on the top of the truck. Benny and I talked about how much fun it would be to use the fire engines to pretend to be fighting a house fire using real water.

As soon as Dad returned to the car, I bombarded him with questions about the fire truck and asked if he thought Santa might bring one to us for Christmas. Noncommittal, our father got back out of the vehicle to read the poster more closely. As we continued into town, Dad told us that he wasn't sure if Santa would bring the fire trucks telling us that $3.98 was a lot of money for a toy. Benny and I both agreed that our hearts were set on getting the shiny new fire trucks for Christmas that year. We continued to express our desire to both Mom and Dad every time that they would lend us an ear. I negotiated with myself hoping that at the very least Santa would bring one red fire engine that Benny and I could share. I experienced sheer joy that December when both my brother and I received a red Texaco fire engine for Christmas. I was in disbelief that I now had my own fire truck and immediately wanted someone to connect the water hose so that I could try out my new toy.

My older sister and brothers usually asked for clothes for Christmas, but sometimes requested games. One Christmas, one received a game of Chinese checkers that I learned to play along with my other siblings. Another Christmas saw a very special and much-desired Christmas gift for my older siblings. A brand-new, shiny 16" Schwinn bicycle arrived at our house. Although the bike had to be shared by the three of them, they nonetheless were ecstatic with being able to ride around the streets of our neighborhood. Johnny took tremendous pride in keeping the bicycle clean and polished and would spend hours shining the chrome fenders and waxing the red and white seat. I would beg my older siblings to let me ride along, sitting on the long bar that extended from the front wheel to the seat of the bike; it was thrilling to feel the wind in my face as one of my older brothers would let the bicycle coast down a long hill.

Mom usually requested something related to our house as a Christmas present. One Christmas Eve, on a very cold day, my Dad and our neighbors were busy installing a new picture window in our living room that was Dad's Christmas gift to my Mom. Although the stove was well-stoked with coal and producing heat, it did not seem to be enough, and I could not get warm. My mother's excitement was contagious and everyone tolerated the cold knowing that it was necessary for Mom to receive her desired gift. It was well after dark when the project was complete, but it did not stop my mother from going in and out of the house into the cold several times to marvel at her beautiful window.

Dad usually would request some sort of new tool or clothes for Christmas. While arriving at my grandparents, one Christmas day in the early 1960s, my father was awestruck when he opened a new Norelco electric razor. Everyone wanted him to try it out immediately in that we had watched advertisements for it on television for the past few weeks. The enjoyable commercial showed Santa sitting on the electric shaver riding down a hill of snow while a lively Christmas song was playing. Mom was so happy for my Dad since he would now be able to save time for shaving each morning before going to work.

One Christmas season, our entire family loaded up the car and drove to Harveytown on a shopping trip. My sister and brothers and I were given one dollar to spend as we pleased; however, Mom dropped several not-so-subtle hints that we might think about using the money to buy gifts for others in keeping with the spirit of the holiday season. I decided to shop the JJ Newberry store to find gifts for Mom and Dad. Looking in unfamiliar areas of the store for my parents' gifts, I began to wonder if I could manage to buy a present for everyone in my family with the single dollar in my pocket. My hunt was on, with my first find being a pair of nylon hosiery for my mother that cost twenty-five cents; then I located a box of three, neatly-pressed handkerchiefs for Dad that would cost another quarter. With fifty-cents remaining, I began to scavenge the toy department for my younger brother; a small plastic car was located for Benny, priced at fifteen-cents. I located pairs of socks for Johnny and Ronnie that would cost an additional ten cents each. I asked a salesclerk to help me locate a present for Debbie that would cost fifteen cents or less, and decided on a miniature bottle of *Evening in Paris* perfume in a cobalt blue bottle that sold for a dime. Taking all the items to the cash register counter to pay, I was excited that I had managed to find something for everyone in my family within the one-dollar budget. Moreover, totaling all the prices in my head, I knew that I would receive a nickel back from the cashier that I could use to buy something for myself at the candy counter. After the salesclerk took my dollar and bagged the items, she returned two cents to me from the cash register. "Don't I get a nickel back?" I asked. The clerk explained to me that I had to pay sales tax on my purchase and that my change of two cents was correct. I did not understand it all but left the store happy and excited that I would surprise my entire family with a gift for Christmas.

In the latter part of the 1960s, I was beginning to lose interest in playing with most of my favorite toys. I no longer played with my cars and trucks under the crawl space of our house, and several of my toys were now broken due to repeated use. My friend, Robby, had gotten a BB gun for Christmas and I quickly realized how much more fun it would be to shoot the long rifle as opposed to playing with my cap pistol. One of my favorite pastimes was to allow a rubber ball to roll down the hill while I engaged in shooting at a moving target. I asked for and received a BB gun of my own as a present and would have fun playing a game of sharp shooting by hanging a target on the side of the privy. I was continuously forewarned by my parents that if I was caught shooting the BB gun at my brothers or any other person or animal, the gun would be broken into pieces and thrown away.

My paternal aunt and uncle would always mail a parcel at Christmastime that contained presents for all my siblings and me. The package would arrive at the Dawson Post Office located a mile or so from our house at the lower end of the community. We kids would make two trips to the post office each day in hopes that the parcel had arrived with the morning or afternoon delivery. One Christmas, my uncle's parcel arrived at my grandparents' house instead of being sent to Dawson. My Papaw opened a package that was tagged for him and discovered a toy robot; Mamaw said he was puzzled, yet amused for a few hours, wondering why his son had sent him a robot for Christmas. The mix-up was straightened out when my younger brother Benny opened a gift tagged for him that contained a man's dress shirt.

Since our family opened gifts on the evening of Christmas Eve, I wanted to spend Christmas day enjoying mine. Often, we would travel to my grandparents' house on Christmas day to enjoy a delicious meal. I usually would take my special gift with me to continue enjoying it and to show it off to my grandparents. Mamaw, with Mom and Debbie's assistance, would spend several hours in the kitchen preparing a delectable baked ham. When the ham came out of the oven, Papaw would be asked to trim away all the fat before my grandmother placed slices of pineapple on its top and returned it to the oven. When the meal was ready and everyone was seated at the table, the ham would be placed in the center for everyone to admire before eating. Bowls of small, boiled potatoes, green beans raised by my grandfather, and hot biscuits would complement the delicious ham. My father's favorite sweet treat, banana pudding, would be served for dessert, capping off the wonderful feast.

After dinner, I would usually take a nap while the dishes were cleaned and put away and the adults and my older siblings watched the television. As we returned home at dusk, I relished in feeling contented and secure.

By the late 1960s, Christmas day would be spent at home, with my mother preparing a wonderful meal. A plump hen would be baked and served with dressing and gravy. Sometimes sweet potatoes would be prepared instead of mashed potatoes, while boiled peas or Brussels sprouts substituted for green beans. The delicious yeast rolls, usually reserved for Sunday dinner, would be baked and a delectable cake would be enjoyed for dessert. Lots of changes in my life had taken place in the latter part of the decade and it was sometimes difficult to allow myself to experience the joy and celebration that Christmas had always brought.

11/Saying Goodbye

The spring of 1964 ushered in an abrupt, unforeseen circumstance for our family. I had heard my mother speak to Momma Poe about Dad having heart damage as the result of a childhood illness; however, I seldom had witnessed my father being ill other than battling an occasional cold or a stomach bug. Dad seemed to be the strong one in our family, the person whom everyone asked for help when a physical task appeared to be overwhelming.

As the end of the school year approached, my father began to struggle just to make it through the workday. Since Benny and I both were now attending Dawson School and my older siblings all were in high school, I only spent time with my father after he returned home from Creekside School each day and on the weekends. One warm spring afternoon I was busy playing on the lawn when I glanced to see Dad park his car in the driveway as he always did while arriving home. I continued to play until I heard my mother call, "Thomas Lee, please come over here now." I ran over and greeted Dad, who had the door open but had not yet gotten out of his car. "I need you to go find your older brothers to help your Dad out of the car and into the house," Mom directed. "Dad, is something wrong?" Are you sick?" I asked. Dad told me that he would be OK in a bit and to run on as my mother had requested I do. I found Johnny and Ronnie listening to records in the basement with a neighbor friend who was visiting. After I relayed Mom's message, my older brothers ran out of the basement and to my father's car. I watched as Dad exited his car, placing his arms around the shoulders of Johnny and Ronnie, and made his way into the house with my brothers' assistance. I kept asking Mom what was wrong with Dad, and she would only tell me not to worry and that my father just needed to rest.

For the next couple of weeks, Dad continued to work and was able to independently get out of his car and go into our house when he arrived home; however, it was obvious to everyone that

Mom was very worried about Dad. I had overheard my mother tell Debbie that she didn't see how Dad continued to walk since his legs and feet stayed so swollen. Dad would lie down on the bed to rest until dinner was ready; after dinner, he would make his way to the privy and then back in the house to prepare for bed. I had overheard my parents discussing Dad's health. Mom insisted that he let her schedule an appointment with the doctor, which he agreed to do.

When Dad returned home after seeing his doctor, he told my mother that his blood pressure was extremely elevated and that he would need to be in the hospital for a few days for testing and evaluation. I had not seen any of my family members hospitalized previously and had lots of questions for Mom with respect to what was happening with my Dad. I did not like coming home from school and not being able to see my father. I found myself becoming anxious and irritable, with the feeling not going away even when I watched a favorite program on television or played in the yard with Benny. I was spending more time after school playing with my friend, Chad, whom Mom continued to watch during the day while his mother worked at the hospital and his Dad was at school. Since Chad would be at our house when we arrived home from school, we would play in our yard until his Mom got home from work; the two of us would then move our playing activities to Chad's house located across the street from us.

A couple of days after Dad had been admitted to the hospital, I arrived home to find my mother sobbing. Mom took me in her arms and told me that Dad's doctor had contacted her and asked her to come to his office for a conference the next afternoon. Mom went on to tell me that she was afraid that the doctor would give her bad news about my father's health. I attempted to console Mom while trying to manage my own anxiety and concern about the news. When my older siblings arrived home from school later, Mom had regained her composure and told Benny and me to go outside to play so she could discuss the matter with them. I ate dinner that evening and then spent the rest of the time trying to finish a library book I had checked out at school and was due back the next day. Although I had been enjoying the book immensely, I had difficulty concentrating and found myself just scanning the words and turning the pages. I thought of Dad as I was trying to go to sleep and wondered if he liked his bed at the hospital.

Mom took the SVTC bus to the hospital for the appointment with Dad's doctor, taking Chad with her. She had made prior arrangements with Chad's Mom for a ride back home at the end of the workday. Everyone was watching from our yard for the Young's Volkswagon Beetle to pull into Chad's driveway. Mom walked slowly across the street after arriving home and made her way into the house. She asked that we all come into the kitchen and take a seat. My mother proceeded to tell us that the doctor had told her that Dad's heart was now considerably weaker due to the damage caused from the childhood illness and that more than likely he would not live much longer. "Oh no!" I screamed. "I don't want my Dad to die," I continued. Everyone had begun to cry while my mother remained strong, trying her best to console her children. I was inconsolable, running to the living room and falling face down on the couch. "My Dad will be OK. He is not going to die," I told myself while continuing to sob. I continued to be distraught for the next few days.

Chad's Mom gave Dad a ride home from the hospital the day he was released. Mom had told everyone that we were not to talk with Dad about what she had told us or to lose our composure since he did not need to be upset; this was extremely difficult for me to do when I saw him. I couldn't imagine the life I knew without my father. Questions such as - "Who will teach me to ride a 16-inch bicycle? Who will take me camping and get me ready to be a Boy Scout? How will I learn to swim? Who will help me with sports as I grow older? Who will put his arm around me and read me a story or sing me a funny song?" raced through my head and I felt insecure that anyone could now answer them. I prayed that God would save my father from death and that I would not see him in a casket like Mrs. Spicer.

I tried my best to be cheerful around my father, spending even more time curling up in the bed with him before I had to return to my bed to sleep. I continued to think about more and more questions that I did not have answers for as Dad would listen to the radio's live broadcast of a call-in talk show during the evenings. Benny would often join Dad and me as we listened to the radio, or my father agreed to turn the radio off and tell us a story. Momma Poe had purchased an electric blanket for Dad after he had told my mother that he was experiencing difficulty keeping his legs and feet warm while he was in bed. I would curl under the warm blanket trying to convince myself that the doctor and what Mom had told me was all wrong and that Dad would get well very soon.

After a week or so, Dad felt well enough to return to school to finish out the year. Only a week or so of school remained and Dad managed to get to and from work without too much difficulty. My father continued to be extremely tired at the end of the day and continued to retire to bed very early in the evening.

My mother had called Mamaw and Papaw Brown to tell them about her visit with Dad's doctor. My grandparents were aware that my father was hospitalized a few days for evaluation but were totally unaware that his heart condition was so dire; Mom told us kids that they were devastated to hear that their son might not have very long to live. My grandparents' visits to our house became more frequent and on occasion Benny and I would return home with them for an overnight visit. Papaw had told me privately that my grandmother's "...nerves were acting up..." and that I should not say anything to her about my Dad that might upset her further.

Dad's health continued to worsen, and my mother was able to secure a hospital bed for my father to use at home. Since my father was spending most of his time lying down, Mom thought the hospital bed would provide more comfort since the back could be raised. Dad spent a lot of time during the day reading old Western dramas written by Zane Grey; he had lost most of his interest in watching television but would still watch a few shows from his bed, which was located in the living room.

Several people, some of whom I knew, came to our house to visit my father over the course of the summer. Both my second and third grade teachers from Creekside School, Miss Morgan and Miss Carnes, visited and brought Benny and me new coloring books. Mrs. Creech, the assistant superintendent of the school district, came and discussed with Dad whether he thought his health would improve enough for him to return to his job in the fall; he told her that he planned to return to work.

This was the first summer that I could remember my father not being away from home to work at the scouting camps. Mom had told everyone that our budget was severely strained without the extra income that our parents had been accustomed to having during the summer. I sensed that my mother was under tremendous strain and stress and had taken notice of her spending much more time working in our yard. My mother always grew beautiful flowers in her garden and around the perimeter of our house each summer and took great pains to make sure they were watered frequently. Tagging along with Mom one evening while she was using the water hose to give her flowers a drink, I mustered up the courage to ask her directly, "Mom, is Dad going to die real soon?" She hesitated before responding and I noticed tears running down her face. "I don't know, honey. Only God knows. We can't lose hope that your Dad will get well and regain his strength."

My sister and brothers and I would talk about our father's illness from time to time, with no resolution ever reached regarding our family's state of flux. One day my sister, Debbie, burst into tears as she rhetorically asked, "What will happen to us if Tom dies?" No one could proffer an answer or provide any reassurance that everything would be just fine.

Debbie was out of high school and had taken a job at a store in Harveytown; she would commute each day riding the SVTC bus. When Debbie returned home from work one afternoon, she was carrying a large bag that she said contained a surprise for Benny and me. Inside the bag was an inflatable swimming pool that we took turns filling with air from our lungs. Mom stretched the water hose across the yard to fill the pool with water while Benny and I changed into old shorts before getting in the water. I was excited to be enjoying the pool and thanked my sister several times for buying it. However, even the pool, which I had dreamed about having, couldn't make my sadness go away.

My older brothers took care of mowing our lawn with a push mower that had a reel of revolving blades that would cut the blades of grass as it was moved back and forth. Before each mowing, Johnny would get a hand file from my father's toolbox in the basement and sharpen each of the blades. Mom would caution my brothers that the grass could not be allowed to grow very tall, or it would be extremely difficult to get the push mover to operate effectively. My brothers also had secured summer jobs from some of our neighbors to paint the outside of their homes. Ronnie complained that one elderly lady was paying him by the hour and would sit on her porch with a clock, deducting the time that he had to climb down and move the ladder. Johnny's interest in girls had intensified and he and other male friends would spend time playing songs about love and romance on Dad's large record player in the basement. I would often listen to the teenage boys talk about their girlfriends.

Ronnie, who had established a reputation as our family's comedian, was aware that we needed as much levity as could be found. He was quite astute at parodying some of our relatives and neighbors in the community and would keep everyone in stitches for hours on end. Dad would sometimes offer a mild reproof when Ronnie was performing, telling him that he shouldn't be garnering laughs at the expense of others; when he continued after my father's criticism, Dad could be seen smiling, trying hard not to break out into laughter.

On a hot August morning, I had walked several streets from my house to visit with two of Mom's sisters, one of whom was visiting from San Francisco. I was watching the morning game shows on television when one of my aunts happened to look out the window seeing Ronnie running down the street. "I think he's crying. I wonder what is wrong?" my aunt said. I continued watching the show until my other aunt came into the room and opened the front door seeing my brother enter the yard. "What's wrong, Ronnie? Is everything OK?" my aunt asked. I heard Ronnie say in a sobbing voice, "No! Tom died!" "What?" my aunt exclaimed ushering Ronnie into the house. "He's dead. He died in his bed. Our neighbors are there, and they've called the funeral home," Ronnie continued. I immediately jumped up from the couch screaming, "No! No! Dad can't be dead! No!" One of my aunts swiftly embraced me as we both stood sobbing.

While Ronnie and I remained distraught, my aunts regained enough presence of mind to decide that we needed to get into the car immediately and drive to my house. My aunt from California drove and spared no time in trying to get to the house as soon as possible. A couple of teenagers were riding their bicycles rather slowing in the street prompting my aunt to lay on the car's horn shouting, "Get out of the road!" When we arrived, everyone quickly exited the car and went into the house. I immediately saw Benny in the kitchen standing alone; my brother and I embraced, and I continued to say, "I can't believe our Dad is dead." I could hear several of my neighbors' voices and began to make my way into the living room to see my father. I was stopped at the kitchen door by Ronnie who abruptly ushered me into the bathroom, shouting, "You can't go in there. You don't need to see Tom dead. You can come out after the undertaker's gone."

I remained in the bathroom screaming to be released as Ronnie held the door closed. I felt totally vulnerable and realized that I had no control over the world as I knew it. "Why is this happening? I want it to stop now! I want everything to go back to being as it always has been. I need someone to help me, please," were the thoughts racing through my head as I continued to sob and plead with my brother to let me see my Dad. It seemed it took forever for the funeral home attendant to arrive and leave the house with my father's body. As soon as Ronnie opened the bathroom door, I bolted from the room, running to the living room. I had secretly hoped that I would see Dad lying in his bed and that I would be able to talk with him.

When I reached the living room, no one was in the bed. The sheet had been taken off, but the pillow remained. As I continued to look at the bed, I thought there were no more tears to come out, yet I continued to bawl. "I want to see my mother," I thought. Mom had gone into town for groceries with Momma Poe and had not yet returned. I thought with horror about my mother learning of my father's death. My brothers and I were still in the living room when I heard Mom's cries in the kitchen. I ran in and my mother embraced me while continuing to sob. Mom kept telling me that she was so sorry that my father had passed and that everything would be fine.

The next morning, one of my mother's sisters drove her to Harveytown to visit the funeral home to make arrangements for Dad's funeral. Benny and I stayed behind, spending most of our time in the basement trying to comfort one another. We noticed that there were several bottles of ginger ale and some other food items that had been left over from our family's July 4th celebration. I went to ask our aunt, who was looking after us, if we could drink some of the soda and eat some of the sweet treats; she gave us permission to do so. Searching for anything that might bring us a little cheer, we partook of the special treats but found very little solace from our indulgence.

My father's funeral was held at the church near our house where Chad's father, Mr. Young, served as part-time pastor. Mom had made sure that everyone in our family wore our Sunday best and that we were well groomed. I overheard my mother's aunts lauding her long, black gloves that she wore with a black dress. Everyone walked to the church and was seated in front for the service. A long casket, a replica of the one I saw at Mrs. Spicer's funeral, was in the front of the church flanked by an abundance of sprays and baskets of colorful flowers. When the service had ended, everyone filed by the coffin to view my father's body. When I saw my father, he appeared to be sleeping. I wanted so much to give him a hug and have him return the embrace, but I resisted. I watched outside the church as my mother and grandparents said goodbye to Dad, saddened that there was nothing I could do to console them.

We followed the hearse to the cemetery where Dad was to be buried. I watched as the coffin remained closed and everyone returned to their cars after the commital service. I looked out the back window of the car until I could no longer see his grave as the vehicle turned onto the highway for the drive back to our house. The rest of my day was spent trying to mask my grief by grazing on some of the food that neighbors had brought to our house.

My Dad's sister from California had attended the funeral and was still visiting at our house. She and her husband recently had traveled to the New York World's Fair and had brought

Benny and me books. My book was a pop-up that displayed the tall buildings in three dimensions and was filled with colorful pages of interesting things. Despite my sadness, I enjoyed talking with my aunt since she had traveled extensively and would tell me about interesting places she had been. She described the Empire State Building in New York City in detail and told me about traveling to the top on an elevator. Dad's brother had attended the funeral service but was unable to stay and visit due to his work obligations in Roanoke.

For several days after my father's funeral, I would find myself searching around the house for anything that might be of interest to me. Benny and I tried playing cars and trucks, but it only reminded me of all the vehicles in our father's funeral procession to the cemetery. Our friend Chad invited us to his house to play in the late afternoon after his mother had returned from work. I noticed that I did seem to feel a little more like myself when I was away from our house for a time. We three boys began to make plans with respect to how we might make improvements to our club house. Benny had seen an old kitchen sink faucet with a knob to turn the water on and off in our basement; we made plans to connect the faucet to a metal container with rubber tubing that would simulate a real sink in our club house.

A month or so after my father's death, Mom and I were sitting on the front porch enjoying a warm summer evening in the swing when we heard a siren in the distance. As the sound grew louder, we saw an ambulance with its red light flashing turn at our street and continue on past our house. Still sensitive to any vehicle resembling a hearse, I asked Mom what might be wrong. She told me that most likely someone was ill and needed to go to the hospital. The next day I learned that a school friend's father had shot himself and that my friend had tried to stop him unsuccessfully. I could not understand why someone would want to harm himself and my mother could not provide any cogent reason other than telling me that there were things in life that could not be understood. Once again, I was forced to confront what seemed like the inescapable reality of death.

12/Transitions

Mom's mother, brothers, and sisters were seen at our house more frequently after Dad's death, assisting my mother with chores and serving as her transportation to Harveytown to shop for groceries and take care of other business. One of my uncles offered to help my mother learn to drive a car. Mom began practicing her driving skills at a county-operated park that had a large shelter house and a graveled road that circled around the facility. Mom would drive around the road in the park over and over and was beginning to build her confidence. Becoming overly self-assured on one of the laps, she increased the speed of the car and then realized that she would not be able to negotiate a curve in the road. She applied the brakes but not before the front fender of the vehicle scraped a wooden post by the road and headed toward the covered shelter, sending people scattering. The mishap was the end of my mother's interest in wanting to learn to drive an automobile.

A stray dog with pronounced black spots on its otherwise white coat of fur began hanging around our house. My sister and brothers and I were secretly feeding the dog scraps from our table and enjoying watching it frolic in the yard. Ronnie and I built up the courage to ask Mom if we could keep the dog since none of our neighbors had told us that the dog belonged to them, expecting her to say, "No." Much to our surprise and delight, our mother agreed to our request and told us that we could keep the dog as our own, unless we discovered that the dog belonged to someone else. We immediately told our siblings the news and a conversation was started about what to name the dog. Ronnie suggested "Freckles," and everyone concurred. Freckles seemed to feel some of my sense of emptiness, and I looked forward to greeting her each day when I would arrive home from school. The dog had full run of our yard, and everyone loved to play chase with Freckles, watching her dart from person to person.

In early fall, my mother had a coal furnace installed in our basement to replace the coal heating stove in our living room.

The business that sold her the furnace took a down payment and allowed for the remaining balance to be paid in installments over time. Mom breathed a profound sigh of relief when the project was completed, knowing how much more efficient the furnace would be in heating our home in the winter. It was decided that Benny and I were now old enough to assist Johnny and Ronnie with the chore of carrying the blocks of coal from the stockpile outdoors using large metal buckets with a funnel-shaped lip. Enough coal would have to be carried to the basement each evening to allow for banking the fire and having enough extra to stoke the coals the next morning. I did not mind carrying the coal into the basement but did not enjoy the chore of shoveling the ashes at the bottom of the furnace into the same buckets and transferring the ash to my mother's flower beds. Our entire family marveled at how much warmer every room in our house felt during the cold winter nights.

An exciting opportunity presented itself when I learned that the church near my home would be sponsoring a Boy Scout troop. A teacher, who lived in the community and had been a member of my father's troop in the early 1950s, had agreed to serve as scout master. Participating in scouting opened up a new world and allowed me to channel much of my grief into a productive, enjoyable activity that paid respect and reverence to my Dad's legacy. My mother agreed to donate a large portion of the scouting equipment that had belonged to my father to the newly-established troop. Each individual scout was asked to go door-to-door in the neighborhood selling items from Tom-Wat kits that would be used to purchase pup tents; enough funds were raised to purchase tents to accommodate all troop members and adult leaders and were used as housing for camping events at Camp Wilderness. My friends and I became very involved in troop activities, earning numerous merit badges to display on our uniforms. Only a year or so after the troop had begun, the scout master moved to North Carolina to a new teaching job and the church was unsuccessful in finding a replacement for him. My fellow scouts and I were crushed that such a fun and gratifying activity was being taken away and that there would be no more excursions to Camp Wilderness where we had roamed the primitive woodlands learning survival skills.

Johnny graduated from high school in the spring of 1964 with plans to enroll in college in the fall. My brother was fortunate to get a summer job at Dawson School assisting a teacher who was teaching summer school. I was saddened to see Johnny go away to college even though we often would argue over usage time of the 16" bicycle, which I could now ride. Johnny returned home on most weekends to have my mother do his laundry and serve him a home-cooked meal.

Benny and I continued to visit with our Mamaw and Papaw. My grandmother's depression stabilized somewhat but she occasionally would break down sobbing and calling my father's name over and over while I was visiting. Sometimes while there, I wished I was back home.

Our neighbors began to invite our family to accompany them on Sunday afternoon excursions. The Youngs would drive us to view the Lonesome Creek Lake and occasionally would take Benny and me along to visit Mrs. Young's parents in Wise. Mr. Young would still take Benny, Chad and me fishing on the lake every now and then, allowing me to see the vast body of water from a different perspective from what I had seen from the shoreline.

The Howard family would invite my family to travel with them to places I had never been. On one trip, we visited the Cumberland Gap National Park and walked to the Pinnacle Overlook where we could view the states of Virginia, Tennessee, and Kentucky simultaneously. Both families packed a picnic basket and we had lunch on the grounds before exploring the forested area's hiking trails.

Out of necessity, Mom began to search for a job outside the home. Benny and I were ambivalent about such a change but were assured by our mother that she would still be available to us as she had been in the past. Fortunately, a part-time store clerk position became available at Dawson Market and my mother was chosen for the job. Initially, it was somewhat of a novelty to walk to the store after school instead of making my way home. I especially looked forward each day to having a variety of snacks from which to choose to satisfy my hunger after a long day at school. Mom seemed to enjoy her job and my siblings and I were glad that she did not seem as sad as we had seen her earlier after my father had died.

One evening Mom came home and told us that she would be going on a date at the end of the week. I was completely taken aback and abruptly told my mother that she should not be going out with another man if she still loved my father; her announcement simultaneously brought intense feelings of anger and sadness. "How could Mom do this to my father?" I thought. Mom informed us that her new friend's name was Bruce Wright and that they were only going into town to have dinner before she returned home. I could not be appeased and told my mother that I would never like Bruce and that I might even throw eggs on his car when he came to our house. I was sternly told by my mother that I had crossed the line with my threat and needed to be quiet. Mom refused to discuss the matter with me further.

Once again, I felt that my life as I knew it had been upended and that I was completely vulnerable. Benny and I would commiserate with each other wondering why we were experiencing all these changes; we both wanted things to go back to being as they were. My older siblings were introduced to Mom's suitor first and reported to Benny and me that he seemed really nice and that they liked him. Ronnie, in particular, tried to reassure us that everything would be fine and that we should give Bruce a chance to be our friend. When Bruce came inside our house for a short visit, Benny and I met him for the first time; I was polite but certainly not amiable. Bruce was a short man with a thinning hairline who looked nothing like my father. Mom had told me that I could call him by his first name after I had told her that I would never call him Dad; the awkwardness of the situation made it much easier for me to now discern why my older siblings had called my Dad "Tom". Bruce had brought us an entire box of candy bars to enjoy, the allure of which competed with my dislike and anger toward the man; he smiled often but did not talk incessantly like my mother sometimes did.

Over the next several months, my mother's courtship with Bruce continued and I got to know him better. Benny and I would go along with Mom and Bruce on rides to Thunder Gap where we would stop at a drive-in restaurant to eat. This was a real treat that I only experienced very infrequently and provided a demonstrative display of Bruce's kindness. When my mother announced that she and Bruce were going to marry, I raised an objection but gave tacit approval since I had grown somewhat fond of Bruce, and realized I had no say in the matter.

Like our mother, who was widowed, Bruce had lost his wife as well. All of Bruce's children were grown and would not be moving to our house. One of the first things Bruce changed when he and Mom married was to subscribe to a newly available television cable service that allowed our television to receive a clear picture and three of the major networks just like what we had been viewing at my grandparents' house for the past several years. Shortly after Bruce subscribed to the cable service, he purchased a new color television set that everyone was excited to watch.

Over the next year, my parents installed a commode in the bathroom and built an additional bedroom. Mom and Bruce occupied the new bedroom and Benny and I now shared the large bedroom that our father had built. My brother and I each had our own twin-size bed and more space than we ever could have imagined. Debbie now had a different job in Harveytown that paid more money and had purchased a clothes dryer for our mother for Christmas. Mom and Bruce soon added an automatic washing machine, and the new conveniences were an unbelievable time saver for my mother, whose home responsibilities still included doing the laundry. Benny and I were surprised to jointly receive a brand new 16" bicycle from our sister as a Christmas gift, which significantly broadened our ability to move about the community. With the new bike, I was able to take a paper route delivering the *Harveytown Echo* and now had money in my pockets to purchase additional snacks at school.

At times, it seemed I had been catapulted into another world that I had not known existed. Although the constant change brought about much that was embraced and welcomed by me, I continued to miss my Dad. It seemed like I was healing inside but not completely. The Christmas season especially flooded my mind with memories of my father. I had grown even fonder of Bruce and now recognized that he not only married my mother but also jointly assumed the obligation of helping raise Benny and me. I was having fewer and fewer occurrences of feeling vulnerable and from time to time could catch glimpses of being safe and grounded once again.

The scope of my world continued to broaden as I now was allowed to visit the Dawson School playground after school to participate in sports and other games. My favorite activity was football, and I loved outrunning my opponent and snagging an over-the-shoulder pass to score a touchdown the way my friend Robby had taught me. Benny played as well, and the game would sometimes change to tackle football without any protective equipment; both of us kept this secret from our mother and managed to escape any serious injury. Benny did sustain a bad injury when he and several other boys decided to pile on our bicycle and ride it down a steep hill; he was sitting on the front fender and was thrown off when the bike's tire ran over a large rock.

Bruce now took us into Harveytown to visit the barber shop on Saturdays. I discovered that I had choices for a haircut other than the buzz cut to which I had grown accustomed. Bruce owned a small business in Harveytown that delivered snack products to service stations and small grocers. Since our grandparents were continuing to age and did not get out as much, Bruce often would drive us to visit with them on early Saturday morning, remaining in town for several hours before picking us back up later in the afternoon for the trip home.

My mother continued to work part-time at Dawson Market seeing many customers and other acquaintances who would wait in the store for the SVTC bus to arrive. A friend had told Mom that a position for a part-time clerk was open at Dawson School. My mother applied and was chosen for the job which paid a much higher wage and had medical insurance and retirement benefits. Although I missed visiting Mom frequently at Dawson Market, I was happy that she was enjoying her new job at the school.

My sister Debbie married in 1968 and she and her husband moved to Charleston, West Virginia. Debbie no longer worked outside the home since her husband had a good job with benefits at a plastics manufacturing plant. Bruce would occasionally drive our family to visit Debbie and her husband on the weekends. A new and much-improved road had been constructed from Harveytown to Cedartown and Interstate 81 could be accessed at Carter's Mill; the interstate continued on to Roanoke and beyond reducing the driving time considerably from when I first traveled to the city with my grandparents. I ate at my first fast food restaurant on one such trip, enjoying both Kentucky Fried Chicken and McDonalds.

Ronnie graduated from high school in the spring of 1968, and continued on to college during the fall of the year. I transitioned from Dawson School to Camden Jr. High and rode the school bus to school for the first time. My new school was a drastic change from elementary school. I now had several teachers throughout the day and had to change classrooms frequently. Camden Jr. High had served as an area high school for several decades before consolidation of several schools took place. The school had a spacious library, a science room with spaces and equipment to complete experiments, and a large cafeteria. A roomy gymnasium was adjacent to the school and had boys' and girls' locker rooms.

Everyone was required to purchase a uniform for physical education class and wear a pair of sneakers that would not scratch the gymnasium floor. The teacher, Mr. Hall, was a military veteran who was both respected and feared. I, along with my classmates, endured a daily regimen of sit-ups, push-ups, and attempting pull-ups. Over the course of one semester, I lost twenty pounds of weight. I decided to enroll in beginning band to learn to play an instrument; one of my aunts had played in her high school band and agreed that I could borrow her instrument. I continued to bring home an honorable report card and my mother and grandparents always looked for my name in the *Harveytown Echo* when the school's honor roll was listed.

Bruce had an interest in fishing just as my grandfather did and enjoyed standing on the banks of the local rivers trying his luck. I had gone along with our family a time or two but could not overcome my impatience with the endless waiting; it did not help matters knowing I had not caught a single fish out of the river. I much preferred to be enjoying the water by swimming in a pool or fishing from a boat on the lake.

One afternoon while Mom, Bruce and I were fishing the river, a truck came speeding down the highway and came to an abrupt stop on the shoulder of the road where Bruce's car was parked. A man exited the truck running toward us yelling, "Help! Help! You all have to help us! We're all shot up and need to get to the hospital. The brakes just went out on my truck, and I cannot drive it." Bruce walked up to the truck to assess the situation, coming back to tell my mother and me that we needed to gather our belongings quickly and get in the car. Two additional passengers got out of the truck; they were having trouble walking and were helped to Bruce's car. A woman sat with Mom and Bruce in the front seat and I was seated between two men sitting in the back of the car. On the way to the hospital, my family learned that the woman in the front of the car was the mother of one man and a sister of the other. Apparently, the two men had gotten into a heated argument which ended in a gun fight outside. The mother stepped between the two men hoping her presence would avert any weapons being used; instead, one of the men shot the woman and then the two men shot each other.

The drive to the hospital was nerve-wracking, with Bruce maintaining his usual calm composure. My mother told me later that day that she was horrified during the entire journey to the medical facility. I remained totally quiet and fearful as the two men with whom I was seated continued to argue with one another. As one of the men exited the car at the hospital and was seated in a wheelchair for transport to the emergency department, he was asked by the attendant how he was feeling. The man replied, "I have so many bullet holes that I feel like a sifter." After my parents and I arrived home, our family spent several hours for the rest of the afternoon cleaning the car using detergent and disinfectants.

Civil unrest across the country continued to grow. The evening news on television captured vivid images of people marching in the streets of large cities to protest the treatment and discrimination of black citizens. My *Weekly Reader* at school was filled with stories and pictures of the civil rights movement which evoked lively discussions in my history class. I now had a clearer understanding of the reason for the unrest and supported the movement, having been an eyewitness to the discrimination experienced by black citizens in my own county. One of my friends at school was a black boy whose family continued to live in the segregated section of the coal camp at Coalgap where my grandparents once lived; occasionally, I would overhear my classmate make fun of him simply because of the color of his skin. I felt embarrassed and ashamed that I had ever participated in using derogatory language about people who were different from me with my friends. In 1968, Dr. Martin Luther King was assassinated while visiting Memphis, Tennessee, to participate in a peaceful protest of black citizens who were being discriminated against in their place of work. I couldn't understand why this happened and had not yet heard anyone provide a tenable reason for the disrespect and denial of equal rights for black citizens.

As the decade began to draw to a close, the conflict in Vietnam continued to escalate. Johnny was drafted into the Army and completed a tour in Vietnam. My brother Ronnie had been continuing with his college studies but concluded that he, too, would be drafted into the military soon; rather than waiting, Ronnie enlisted in the Army and completed his basic training. Shortly thereafter, he was deployed to Vietnam to serve in the infantry. Our family continued to face even more heightened worry and anxiety about the safety of our members. Just as with Johnny, letters served as our only mechanism to communicate with Ronnie.

On a hot, late summer day, military officers came to our house to inform my mother that Ronnie had been killed in action in Vietnam. Once again, death had invaded our family and I found myself experiencing the loss of someone whom I deeply loved. My bereavement was further compounded by my mother's profound grief. Bruce became the stabilizing rock in our family, always showing patience and trying very hard to help everyone move forward with life.

As the 1960s were coming to an end, there was one thing that I now knew for certain. Love, loss, and change would continue to be a part of my life that required my engagement and acceptance. I discovered that I had unmasked my resilience and ability to survive regardless of any abrupt, unanticipated change in my life. I tried not to speculate too intently about the future, thinking it best to let events unfold at their discretion. I would be transitioning to high school the next year and was aware that my studies would increase in difficulty if I was serious with respect to preparing myself for college; my parents had told me from a young age that I would not be finished with school until I had finished college and that thought and objective had stuck with me throughout the years. I did think from time to time whether, I, just as my brothers and other relatives, would serve in the military and be deployed to a warzone. "I might even die while fighting," I sometimes mused.

What the 1970s would hold in store for me, I didn't know and I tried my best to avoid thinking too much about the matter, choosing instead to revel in spending time with my family and friends and pursuing my interests and hobbies. Time had meted out to me significant loss that had left a metaphorical hole in my heart and yet I still felt equipped with unfathomable love from my family to journey forward with my life.

www.ingramcontent.com/pod-product-compliance
Lightning Source LLC
LaVergne TN
LVHW042115190726
843493LV00006B/1486